diabetic LIVING Everyday COOKING

VOLUME 7

DIABETIC LIVING® EVERYDAY COOKING
IS PART OF A BOOK SERIES PUBLISHED BY
BETTER HOMES AND GARDENS SPECIAL
INTEREST MEDIA, DES MOINES, IOWA

Pork, Sweet Potato, and
Apple Salad with Greens
recipe on page 52

Serving healthful meals my family will like

is one of my daily goals, and it's often my biggest challenge. Our schedules are packed with work and after-school activities, so I try to organize weekly menus and shop for the majority of groceries on weekends. I have my standard go-tos, but I'm constantly looking for new ideas. That's why I welcome this new edition of lightened-up recipes, each with complete nutritional analysis and diabetic exchanges, to my cookbook repertoire.

Because our registered dietitians have fine-tuned every recipe, I know each one delivers healthful amounts of calories, carb, fats, and sodium. And the Better Homes and Gardens® Test Kitchen seal of approval assures me that every recipe has been tested for accuracy and ease of preparation. They also taste great. I know because I often taste them (just a tiny bite or I'd be in big trouble). To make meal prep easy, look for helpful shopping strategies, ingredient swaps, flavor variations, and simple serving ideas throughout this book.

Turn to page 108 for easy everyday breakfast fare and brunch-style weekend meals or to page 6 for sizzlin' grilled entrées and great stir-fries. There are some fabulous and fresh sandwiches beginning on page 78. Beyond main dishes, this new volume offers everything from soups and easy side dishes to quick snacks and sweet treats. I know you—and your entire family—will love these balanced, nutritious meals.

Here's to healthful eating!

Martha

Martha Miller Johnson
Editor, *Diabetic Living*® magazine

ON THE COVER:

Apricot-Vanilla Clafoutis
recipe on page 148

Photographer: Jason Donnelly

diabetic LIVING Everyday COOKING VOLUME 7

CONSUMER MARKETING

Vice President, Consumer Marketing	JANET DONNELLY
Consumer Marketing Product Director	HEATHER SORENSEN
Consumer Marketing Product Manager	WENDY MERICAL
Business Director	RON CLINGMAN
Production Manager	AL RODRUCK
Contributing Project Manager	SHELLI McCONNELL, PURPLE PEAR PUBLISHING, INC.
Contributing Photographer	JASON DONNELLY
Contributing Food Stylist	JENNIFER PETERSON
Test Kitchen Director	LYNN BLANCHARD
Test Kitchen Product Supervisors	JANE BURNETT, RD, LD; CARLA CHRISTIAN, RD, LD
Editorial Assistants	LORI EGGERS, MARLENE TODD

SPECIAL INTEREST MEDIA

Editorial Director	JIM BLUME
Art Director	GENE RAUCH
Managing Editor	DOUG KOUMA

DIABETIC LIVING® MAGAZINE

Editor	MARTHA MILLER JOHNSON
Art Director	MICHELLE BILYEU
Senior Editor, Food & Nutrition	JESSIE SHAFER
Degital Editor	LORI BROOKHART-SCHERVISH
Assistant Art Director, Health	NIKKI SANDERS

MEREDITH NATIONAL MEDIA GROUP

President **TOM HARTY**

Chairman and Chief Executive Officer **STEPHEN M. LACY**

Vice Chairman **MELL MEREDITH FRAZIER**

In Memoriam — E.T. MEREDITH III (1933-2003)

Diabetic Living® Everyday Cooking is part of a series published by Meredith Corp., 1716 Locust St., Des Moines, IA 50309-3023.

If you have comments or questions about the editorial material in *Diabetic Living® Everyday Cooking*, write to the editor of *Diabetic Living* magazine, Meredith Corp., 1716 Locust St., Des Moines, IA 50309-3023. Send an e-mail to diabeticlivingmeredith.com or call 800/678-2651. magazine is available by subscription or on the newsstand. To order a subscription to magazine, go to *DiabeticLivingOnline.com*

contents

Tiramisu Brownie Parfaits
recipe on page 151

family-pleasing
dinners

When you have the just-right recipes and good-for-you

ingredients, it's easy to cook healthful, family-friendly meals.

Pull together the fresh fixin's and make these easy-to-follow

recipes—stir-fried, grilled, simmered, or baked, each has been

made better for you.

Grilled Steaks with Roasted Garlic

Roasting turns the garlic into a soft, butterlike spread with a sweet, mellow flavor. As the garlic roasts, the olive oil becomes infused with fresh herb flavor, too.

>> SERVINGS 6 (3 ounces cooked steak each)
CARB. PER SERVING 2 g
PREP 20 minutes
GRILL 30 minutes

- 1   whole bulb garlic
- 3   to 4 teaspoons snipped fresh basil or 1 teaspoon dried basil, crushed
- 1   tablespoon snipped fresh rosemary or 1 teaspoon dried rosemary, crushed
- 2   tablespoons olive oil or vegetable oil
- 1½ pounds boneless beef ribeye steaks or sirloin steak, cut 1 inch thick
- 1   to 2 teaspoons cracked black pepper
- ½   teaspoon salt

1 Peel away the dry outer layers of skin from the garlic bulb, leaving skins and cloves intact. Cut off the pointed top portion (about ¼ inch), leaving bulb intact but exposing the individual cloves.

2 Fold a 20x18-inch piece of heavy foil in half crosswise; trim to make a double-thick 10-inch square. Place garlic bulb, cut side up, in the center of foil. Sprinkle with basil and rosemary; drizzle with oil. Bring up two opposite edges of foil; seal with a double fold. Fold the remaining ends to completely enclose garlic, leaving space for steam to build.

3 For a charcoal or gas grill, place garlic in foil packet on the grill rack directly over medium heat. Cover and grill about 30 minutes or until garlic is soft when packet is squeezed, turning occasionally during grilling.

4 Meanwhile, trim fat from steaks. Sprinkle the pepper and salt evenly over all sides of steaks; rub in with your fingers. While garlic grills, add steaks to grill. Cover and grill until steaks reach desired doneness, turning once halfway through grilling time. For ribeye steaks, allow 10 to 12 minutes for medium rare (145°F) or 12 to 15 minutes for medium (160°F). For sirloin steak, allow 14 to 18 minutes for medium rare (145°F) or 18 to 22 minutes for medium (160°F).

5 Remove garlic from foil, reserving basil mixture. Squeeze garlic pulp onto steaks. Mash pulp slightly, spreading it over steaks. To serve, cut steaks into six serving-size pieces. Drizzle steaks with the reserved basil mixture.

PER SERVING: 225 cal., 13 g total fat (4 g sat. fat), 75 mg chol., 259 mg sodium, 2 g carb. (0 g fiber, 0 g sugars), 25 g pro. Exchanges: 3.5 lean meat, 1 fat.

2 grams carb.

Garlic-Lime Skirt Steak with Grilled Tomato-Pepper Chutney

Skirt steak is traditionally thinner than flank steak. If you use flank steak that is thicker than $^3/_4$ inch, make sure to cook it a few minutes longer.

SERVINGS 8 (3 ounces steak and 3 tablespoons chutney each)
CARB. PER SERVING 10 g
PREP 20 minutes
MARINATE 2 hours
STAND 35 minutes
GRILL 15 minutes

- 2 pounds beef skirt or flank steak, cut $^1/_2$ to $^3/_4$ inch thick
- 2 tablespoons lime juice
- 2 tablespoons balsamic vinegar
- 2 tablespoons minced garlic (12 cloves)
- 1 tablespoon vegetable oil
- 1 teaspoon coarse salt
- $^1/_2$ teaspoon black pepper
- $^1/_3$ cup finely snipped fresh cilantro
- 8 to 10 miniature sweet peppers
- 1 recipe Grilled Tomato-Pepper Chutney

PER SERVING: 245 cal., 11 g total fat (4 g sat. fat), 74 mg chol., 473 mg sodium, 10 g carb. (2 g fiber, 6 g sugars), 25 g pro. Exchanges: 2 vegetable, 3 lean meat, 1 fat.

1 | Trim fat from steak. Place steak in a large resealable plastic bag set in a shallow dish. In a small bowl whisk together lime juice, vinegar, garlic, oil, salt, and black pepper. Stir in cilantro. Pour over steak in bag; seal bag. Turn to coat. Marinate in the refrigerator for 2 to 24 hours, turning bag occasionally. Drain steak, discarding marinade. Allow steak to stand at room temperature for 30 minutes.

2 | For a charcoal or gas grill, place steak on the grill rack directly over medium-high heat. Cover and grill for 10 to 12 minutes or until internal temperature registers 145°F for medium rare, turning once halfway through grilling time. Let steak stand 5 minutes; thinly slice.

3 | While steak stands, place the miniature sweet peppers on the grill rack directly over medium heat. Grill about 5 minutes or until lightly charred, turning frequently. Serve sliced steak with the grilled peppers and the Grilled Tomato-Pepper Chutney.

GRILLED TOMATO-PEPPER CHUTNEY: For a charcoal or gas grill, place 1 large yellow sweet pepper on the grill rack directly over medium heat. Cover and grill about 15 minutes or until skin is charred and pepper is tender, turning often to evenly char the skin. Remove from grill and wrap pepper in foil. Let stand about 15 minutes or until cool enough to handle. Using a sharp knife, loosen the edges of the skin from the pepper. Gently and slowly pull off the skin in strips; discard skin. Chop pepper; set aside. Seed and chop 2 medium tomatoes. In a 9-inch round disposable foil pan combine the tomatoes, $^1/_2$ cup chopped onion, $^1/_2$ teaspoon salt, and $^1/_4$ to $^1/_2$ teaspoon crushed red pepper. Cover tightly with foil. Place pan on the grill rack directly over medium heat; cover and grill for 20 minutes. Remove foil. Stir in the reserved chopped sweet pepper, 2 tablespoons snipped fresh cilantro, and 1 tablespoon honey. Grill, uncovered, about 5 minutes more or until most of the liquid has evaporated. Transfer to a serving bowl. Cool about 30 minutes or until chutney is at room temperature before serving.

Philly Cheesesteak Burritos

If some like their food peppery hot and some do not, let each diner add the hot pepper sauce at the table.

SERVINGS 4 (1 burrito each)
CARB. PER SERVING 31 g
PREP 40 minutes
FREEZE 30 minutes

- 1 pound beef top round steak
- 2 teaspoons flour
- ¼ teaspoon dry mustard
- ½ cup fat-free milk
- 1 ounce reduced-fat provolone cheese, torn into pieces (1 to 2 slices)
- 2 tablespoons grated Parmesan cheese
- 1 teaspoon olive oil
- 1 8-ounce package sliced fresh mushrooms, such as shiitake, button, or cremini
- 1 large onion, thinly sliced
- 1 medium red sweet pepper, cut into thin strips
- 1 medium yellow sweet pepper, cut into thin strips
- ½ to 1 teaspoon bottled hot pepper sauce
- 4 8- to 9-inch low-carb whole wheat flour tortillas, such as La Tortilla Factory Smart & Delicious brand

PER SERVING: 329 cal., 11 g total fat (3 g sat. fat), 65 mg chol., 488 mg sodium, 31 g carb. (14 g fiber, 8 g sugars), 39 g pro. Exchanges: 2 vegetable, 1 starch, 4.5 lean meat.

1 Trim fat from meat. Partially freeze meat. Thinly slice across the grain into bite-size strips.

2 Meanwhile, prepare cheese sauce. In a small saucepan combine flour and dry mustard. Gradually add milk, stirring with a whisk until blended. Cook and stir until mixture comes to boiling; reduce heat. Cook and stir for 1 minute or until slightly thickened. Gradually add cheeses, stirring until smooth. Remove from heat; cover and keep warm. The mixture will thicken as it cools.

3 In a very large skillet heat oil over medium-high heat. Add half of the meat; cook and stir about 3 minutes or until slightly pink in center. Remove with a slotted spoon. Repeat with remaining meat; remove. Add mushrooms, onion, half of the red pepper strips, and half of the yellow pepper strips to skillet; cook and stir about 4 minutes or just until vegetables are tender. Return all of the meat to skillet. Season mixture with hot pepper sauce.

4 To assemble, spoon about 1¼ cups of the meat mixture onto each tortilla. Top with about 2 tablespoons of the cheese sauce. Fold bottom edge of tortilla up and over filling. Fold in one opposite side; roll up from the bottom. If necessary, secure with toothpicks. Serve with remaining sweet pepper strips.

MAKE-AHEAD DIRECTIONS: Prepare and assemble as directed. Wrap each burrito in plastic wrap and chill for up to 2 hours. To serve, unwrap burrito and place burrito on a microwave-safe plate. Microwave on 70 percent power (medium-high) about 2½ minutes or until heated through.

Braised Beef over Butternut Squash Polenta

If you have a favorite, use a whole turnip or a whole rutabaga instead of the combination of the two.

SERVINGS 6 (1 cup meat-vegetable mixture and $^1/_3$ cup polenta each)
CARB. PER SERVING 31 g
PREP 30 minutes
BAKE 2 hours
COOK 25 minutes

2 pounds boneless beef chuck shoulder pot roast

4 teaspoons olive oil

2 stalks celery, cut into 2-inch pieces

2 medium carrots, cut into 2-inch pieces

2 medium parsnips (about 12 ounces), peeled and cut into 2-inch pieces

$^1/_2$ cup coarsely chopped onion

$^1/_2$ of a medium turnip, peeled and cut into 2-inch pieces

$^1/_2$ of a small rutabaga, peeled and cut into 2-inch pieces

$^1/_2$ cup dry red wine or 50% less-sodium beef broth

2 teaspoons snipped fresh rosemary

$1^1/_2$ cups water

1 cup 50% less-sodium beef broth

2 teaspoons Kitchen Bouquet

$^1/_3$ cup fat-free milk

$^1/_4$ cup water

1 cup cold water

$^3/_4$ cup yellow cornmeal

$^1/_2$ of a 10-ounce package frozen butternut squash ($^2/_3$ cup), thawed

$^1/_2$ teaspoon salt

$^1/_4$ teaspoon black pepper

$^1/_4$ cup cold water

$1^1/_2$ tablespoons flour

Fresh parsley leaves

1 | Preheat oven to 325°F. Trim fat from beef. Cut meat into $1^1/_2$-inch pieces. In an ovenproof 4-quart Dutch oven heat 2 teaspoons of the oil over medium heat. Brown meat, half at a time, stirring frequently. Remove meat from Dutch oven.

2 | In the same Dutch oven cook celery, carrots, parsnips, onion, turnip, and rutabaga in the remaining 2 teaspoons oil for 5 to 7 minutes or until vegetables start to brown. Remove from heat. Stir in wine and rosemary. Add the $1^1/_2$ cups water, beef broth, and Kitchen Bouquet; cook and stir over medium heat until boiling, stirring to scrape up any browned bits from bottom of Dutch oven.

3 | Return meat to Dutch oven. Bake, covered, about 2 hours or until meat is tender.

4 | Meanwhile, for polenta, in a medium saucepan combine milk and the $^1/_4$ cup water; bring to boiling. In a medium bowl stir together the 1 cup cold water and cornmeal. Slowly add the cornmeal mixture to the boiling milk mixture. Reduce heat to medium-low. Stir in squash, salt, and pepper. Cook for 25 to 30 minutes or until mixture is very thick and soft, stirring frequently and adjusting heat as needed to maintain a slow boil.

5 | Stir together $^1/_4$ cup cold water and flour. Add to meat mixture. Cook and stir over medium heat until thickened and bubbly; cook and stir for 1 minute more.

6 | Spoon polenta into shallow serving bowls. Top with meat and vegetables. Sprinkle with parsley leaves.

PER SERVING: 379 cal., 11 g total fat (4 g sat. fat), 100 mg chol., 430 mg sodium, 31 g carb. (4 g fiber, 7 g sugars), 36 g pro. Exchanges: 2 starch, 4 lean meat, 2 fat.

QUICK TIP
When butternut or acorn squash is in season, substitute cooked fresh squash for the frozen option.

Meat Loaf with Sour Cream-Mushroom Sauce

A serrated knife is the perfect choice for cutting the cooked, soft loaf into thin slices.

SERVINGS 6 (3 ounces meat loaf and $\frac{1}{4}$ cup sauce each)

CARB. PER SERVING 10 g

PREP 35 minutes

BAKE 1 hour

STAND 10 minutes

- $\frac{1}{3}$ cup fat-free milk
- 2 egg whites
- 1 cup soft whole grain bread crumbs (1$\frac{1}{3}$ slices bread)
- $\frac{1}{4}$ cup chopped green onions
- 2 teaspoons dried Italian seasoning, crushed
- $\frac{1}{4}$ teaspoon salt
- $\frac{1}{8}$ teaspoon black pepper
- 1 pound 95% lean ground beef
- Nonstick cooking spray
- 1 tablespoon butter
- 1$\frac{1}{2}$ cups sliced fresh mushrooms
- 1 clove garlic, minced
- $\frac{1}{4}$ cup thinly sliced green onions (2)
- 1 8-ounce carton light sour cream
- 2 tablespoons flour
- $\frac{3}{4}$ cup cold water
- 2 teaspoons instant beef bouillon granules
- Sliced green onions (optional)
- Black pepper (optional)

PER SERVING: 214 cal., 10 g total fat (5 g sat. fat), 65 mg chol., 534 mg sodium, 10 g carb. (1 g fiber, 2 g sugars), 21 g pro. Exchanges: 0.5 starch, 3 lean meat, 1 fat.

1 | Preheat oven to 350°F. Line a 2-quart rectangular baking dish with foil; set aside.

2 | In a large bowl combine milk and egg whites; beat with a fork until well mixed. Stir in bread crumbs, $\frac{1}{4}$ cup chopped green onions, the Italian seasoning, salt, and the $\frac{1}{8}$ teaspoon pepper. Add ground beef; mix well. Shape beef mixture into a 7x4-inch rectangle in the prepared baking dish.

3 | Bake about 1 hour or until internal temperature reaches 160°F.* Spoon off fat. Let meat loaf stand for 10 minutes. Using two spatulas, carefully transfer meat loaf to serving platter, draining off as much fat as possible.

4 | Meanwhile, for sauce, coat an unheated medium skillet with cooking spray. Add butter; melt over medium heat. Add mushrooms and garlic; cook about 4 minutes or until mushrooms are nearly tender. Stir in $\frac{1}{4}$ cup sliced green onions; cook for 1 minute more. In a small bowl stir together sour cream and flour. Stir the cold water and beef bouillon granules into the mushroom mixture. Stir sour cream mixture into mushroom mixture in skillet. Cook and stir until thickened and bubbly. Cook and stir for 1 minute more. Add additional water if needed to thin to desired consistency. Serve sauce over meat loaf. If desired, sprinkle with additional sliced green onions and pepper.

*TEST KITCHEN TIP: The internal color of a meat loaf is not a reliable doneness indicator. A beef loaf cooked to 160°F is safe, regardless of color. To measure the doneness of a meat loaf, insert an instant-read thermometer into the center of the loaf.

Zesty Meat Sauce with Spaghetti Squash

Spaghetti squash is higher in nutritents and lower in carbohydrate than pasta, so it's a healthful option when serving flavorful Italian meat sauces.

SERVINGS 6 (³⁄4 cup meat mixture and ³⁄4 cup squash mixture each)
CARB. PER SERVING 21 g
PREP 50 minutes
BAKE 45 minutes

1   medium spaghetti squash
    (about 2¹⁄2 pounds)

1   medium red or green sweet pepper
    (or half of each), cut into thin strips

4   ounces fresh mushrooms, halved
    or quartered

1   small onion, cut into thin wedges

Nonstick cooking spray

12 ounces 95% lean ground beef

¹⁄2 cup chopped onion

¹⁄2 cup chopped carrot

¹⁄2 cup chopped celery

2   cloves garlic, minced

2   8-ounce cans no-salt-added
    tomato sauce

1   cup salsa*

1   cup water

1   tablespoon dried Italian seasoning,
    crushed

¹⁄4 teaspoon black pepper

¹⁄8 to ¹⁄4 teaspoon crushed red pepper

¹⁄4 cup finely shredded Parmesan
    cheese (1 ounce)

1 | Preheat oven to 350°F. Line a 15×10×1-inch baking pan with foil. Halve squash lengthwise. Remove seeds. Place squash, cut sides down, in prepared baking pan. Using a fork, prick the skin all over. Arrange sweet pepper, mushrooms, and onion wedges around squash. Coat vegetables with cooking spray. Bake for 45 to 55 minutes or until squash is tender.

2 | Meanwhile, for meat sauce, in a large skillet combine ground beef, chopped onion, carrot, celery, and garlic. Cook until meat is browned and vegetables are tender, using a wooden spoon to break up meat as it cooks. Drain well.

3 | Stir tomato sauce, salsa, the water, Italian seasoning, black pepper, and crushed red pepper into meat mixture in skillet. Bring to boiling; reduce heat. Simmer, uncovered, for 10 to 15 minutes or until desired consistency, stirring occasionally.

4 | Using a fork, remove the squash pulp from the shells. Spoon 4 cups squash pulp into a large bowl. (Store any leftover squash in a covered container in the refrigerator for up to 3 days.) Toss squash pulp in bowl with the roasted sweet pepper strips, mushrooms, and onion wedges. Serve meat sauce over squash-vegetable mixture. Sprinkle with cheese.

*TEST KITCHEN TIP: Read the nutritional facts on the labels of the salsas available at your grocery store and choose the salsa that's lowest in sodium. Newman's Own Mild Salsa is a good choice.

PER SERVING: 181 cal., 4 g total fat (2 g sat. fat), 37 mg chol., 236 mg sodium, 21 g carb. (6 g fiber, 11 g sugars), 16 g pro. Exchanges: 1 vegetable, 1 starch, 2 lean meat.

4 grams fat

Cocoa Roasted Pork with Wilted Kale

A spicy mocha-flavor mixture creates a delicious crust on the pork tenderloin. It pairs perfectly with the slightly sweet kale mixture.

SERVINGS 4 (3 ounces cooked pork and ³/4 cup kale mixture each)
CARB. PER SERVING 29 g
PREP 25 minutes
ROAST 20 minutes
STAND 3 minutes

- 1   cup water
- 1   tablespoon packed brown sugar*
- 1   teaspoon instant espresso coffee powder
- 1   teaspoon unsweetened cocoa powder
- ½   teaspoon ground ancho chile pepper
- ¼   teaspoon salt
- 1   1-pound pork tenderloin
- 1   tablespoon olive oil
- 1   medium red sweet pepper, cut into thin bite-size strips
- 1   large onion, thinly sliced
- 12 cups coarsely chopped, trimmed kale
- ¼   teaspoon salt

PER SERVING: 286 cal., 7 g total fat (1 g sat. fat), 70 mg chol., 429 mg sodium, 29 g carb. (6 g fiber, 11 g sugars), 30 g pro. Exchanges: 3 vegetable, 0.5 starch, 3 lean meat, 0.5 fat.

1 Preheat oven to 425°F. Place a rack in a shallow roasting pan. Add the water to the pan; set aside. In a small bowl combine brown sugar, coffee powder, cocoa powder, ancho chile pepper, and ¼ teaspoon salt. Trim fat from pork. Sprinkle sugar mixture evenly over pork; rub in with your fingers. Place pork on the rack in the prepared pan.

2 Roast for 20 to 30 minutes or until an instant-read thermometer inserted in center of the pork registers 145°F. Cover pork with foil. Let stand for 3 minutes before slicing.

3 Meanwhile, in a Dutch oven heat oil over medium heat. Add sweet pepper and onion and cook about 5 minutes or until crisp-tender, stirring occasionally. Add kale; sprinkle with the remaining ¼ teaspoon salt. Cook for 3 to 5 minutes or until kale is tender, tossing with tongs so kale cooks evenly. Thinly slice pork. Serve with kale mixture.

*TIEST KITCHEN TIP: We do not recommend using a sugar substitute for this recipe.

Pork Tenderloin with Cucumber-Mango Salad

You can substitute fresh-picked ripe and juicy peaches or nectarines for the mango.

SERVINGS 4 (3 slices cooked pork and ½ cup salad each)
CARB. PER SERVING 18 g
PREP 10 minutes
ROAST 25 minutes
STAND 3 minutes

- 2 tablespoons packed brown sugar*
- 2 teaspoons five-spice powder
- ½ teaspoon salt
- 2 12-ounce pork tenderloins
- 4 green onions
- 1 mango, peeled, seeded, and chopped
- 1 small English cucumber, thinly sliced
- 1 fresh jalapeño chile pepper, stemmed, seeded, and sliced** (optional)

PER SERVING: 266 cal., 6 g total fat (2 g sat. fat), 105 mg chol., 365 mg sodium, 18 g carb. (2 g fiber, 15 g sugars), 35 g pro. Exchanges: 0.5 fruit, 0.5 carb., 4.5 lean meat.

1 Preheat oven to 425°F. Line a shallow roasting pan with foil; set aside. In a small bowl combine brown sugar, five-spice powder, and salt; set 1 teaspoon of the brown sugar mixture aside. Sprinkle the remaining brown sugar mixture evenly over pork tenderloins; rub in with your fingers. Place tenderloins in prepared roasting pan.

2 Roast about 25 minutes or until an instant-read thermometer inserted in centers of pork tenderloins registers 145°F. Cover with foil; let stand for 3 minutes before slicing.

3 Meanwhile, for mango salad, slice the green portions of the green onions into thin strips; chop the white portions. In a medium bowl combine all of the green onions, the mango, cucumber, chile pepper (if desired), and the reserved brown sugar mixture. Slice pork and serve with mango salad.

*SUGAR SUBSTITUTE: Use Sugar Twin Granulated Brown. Follow package directions to use product amount equivalent to 2 tablespoons brown sugar.

**TEST KITCHEN TIP: Because chile peppers contain volatile oils that can burn your skin and eyes, avoid direct contact with them as much as possible. When working with chile peppers, wear plastic or rubber gloves. If your bare hands do touch the peppers, wash your hands and nails well with soap and warm water.

Caramelized Pork with Melon Relish

A head of napa cabbage is quite large. Use the extra soft and ruffled cabbage leaves in salads, stir-fries, or as healthful sandwich wraps.

SERVINGS 4 (1 pork chop, $^1\!/_2$ cup cabbage, and about $^1\!/_2$ cup relish each)
CARB. PER SERVING 20 g
START TO FINISH 25 minutes

- 1 small cantaloupe
- $^1\!/_4$ cup orange juice
- 3 tablespoons hoisin sauce
- 4 5- to 6-ounce center-cut bone-in pork chops, cut $^1\!/_2$ inch thick
- $^1\!/_4$ teaspoon salt
- $^1\!/_8$ teaspoon black pepper
- 2 teaspoons vegetable oil
- 6 tablespoons thinly sliced green onions
- 2 cups shredded napa cabbage

1 Remove rind and seeds from cantaloupe; chop melon. Place 2 cups of the chopped melon in a food processor or blender; add orange juice, Cover and process until smooth. Transfer $^1\!/_2$ cup of the pureed melon to a small bowl; stir in hoisin sauce. Strain the remaining pureed melon, reserving the juice and discarding the solids.

2 Sprinkle chops with the salt and pepper; brush both sides of chops generously with the hoisin sauce mixture. In a very large skillet heat oil over medium heat. Add chops; cook for 5 to 7 minutes or until well browned, slightly pink in centers, and juices run clear, turning once halfway through cooking time.

3 Meanwhile, combine the remaining chopped melon, the strained juice, and green onions. Remove chops from skillet; add the remaining hoisin sauce mixture to skillet. Cook and stir until heated through. Spoon onto four dinner plates. Divide cabbage among plates. Place a chop on each plate. Add melon mixture to skillet to warm slightly. Spoon over chops and cabbage.

PER SERVING: 277 cal., 12 g total fat (2 g sat. fat), 54 mg chol., 413 mg sodium, 20 g carb. (2 g fiber, 16 g sugars), 21 g pro. Exchanges: 1 vegetable, 1 fruit, 3 lean meat, 1 fat.

21 grams pro.

Orange-Sauced Pork Chops with Quinoa

Use an instant-read thermometer to get a quick temp on the pork chops. If you don't have one, the chops are done when centers are slightly pink.

SERVINGS 4 (1 pork chop, 1/3 cup quinoa mixture, and 1 tablespoon sauce each)
CARB. PER SERVING 30 g
PREP 15 minutes
COOK 10 minutes
BROIL 9 minutes
STAND 3 minutes

1 cup reduced-sodium chicken broth

1/2 teaspoon finely shredded orange peel (set aside)

1/3 cup orange juice

2/3 cup quinoa, rinsed and well drained

2 tablespoons sliced green onion

4 5- to 6-ounce bone-in pork loin chops, cut 3/4 inch thick

1/3 cup reduced-sugar orange marmalade

1 tablespoon orange juice or water

2 teaspoons reduced-sodium soy sauce

1/8 teaspoon ground ginger

Orange slices (optional)

1 | Preheat broiler. In a small saucepan combine broth and the 1/3 cup orange juice. Bring to boiling. Slowly add the quinoa and return to boiling; reduce heat. Simmer, covered, for 10 to 15 minutes or until most of the liquid is absorbed and quinoa is tender. Stir in orange peel and green onion.

2 | Meanwhile, place pork chops on the unheated rack of a broiler pan. Broil 3 to 4 inches from the heat for 9 to 10 minutes or until done (145°F), turning once halfway through broiling time. Let stand 3 minutes before serving.

3 | For sauce, in another small saucepan stir together orange marmalade, the 1 tablespoon orange juice, the soy sauce, and ginger. Cook and stir until boiling. Serve sauce with chops and quinoa mixture. If desired, garnish plate with orange slices.

PER SERVING: 324 cal., 11 g total fat (2 g sat. fat), 53 mg chol., 282 mg sodium, 30 g carb. (2 g fiber, 11 g sugars), 24 g pro. Exchanges: 1.5 starch, 0.5 carb., 3 lean meat, 1 fat.

QUICK TIP
Fire up the grill and put these lean and tender chops on the rack for a fast sizzle. They will grill in the same amount of time as they broil.

Blue Cheese-Topped Pork Chops

Some reduced-fat blue cheeses do not crumble as easily as full-fat cheeses, so you may need to use a small spoon to break up the cheese.

SERVINGS 4 (1 pork chop, 2 tomato slices, and 1 tablespoon blue cheese each)
CARB. PER SERVING 2 g
PREP 15 minutes
BROIL 8 minutes
STAND 3 minutes

2 tablespoons bottled fat-free Italian salad dressing

Cayenne pepper

4 5- to 6-ounce bone-in pork loin chops

1 roma tomato, cut into 8 slices

¼ cup crumbled reduced-fat blue cheese (1 ounce)

1 tablespoon snipped fresh rosemary

1 Preheat broiler. In a small bowl combine salad dressing and cayenne pepper. Brush salad dressing mixture over all sides of the pork chops. Place pork chops on the unheated rack of a broiler pan. Broil 3 to 4 inches from heat for 8 to 10 minutes or until done (145°F), turning once halfway through broiling time. Let stand 3 minutes before serving

2 To serve, arrange two tomato slices on each chop. Sprinkle blue cheese over chops and tomatoes. Sprinkle with rosemary.

PER SERVING: 194 cal., 10 g total fat (3 g sat. fat), 57 mg chol., 222 mg sodium, 2 g carb. (0 g fiber, 1 g sugars), 21 g pro. Exchanges: 3 lean meat, 1 fat.

Corn- and Chorizo-Stuffed Poblanos with Green Chile-Cheese Sauce

The size of poblano chiles can vary. Use the scale in the produce department to help select peppers that are large enough to cradle the zippy filling.

SERVINGS 4 (1 stuffed pepper and
¹/₄ cup sauce each)
CARB. PER SERVING 28 g
PREP 25 minutes
BROIL 10 minutes
STAND 20 minutes
BAKE 20 minutes

4   large fresh poblano chile peppers
    (5 to 6 ounces each)

Nonstick cooking spray

8   ounces extra-lean ground pork or
    ground turkey breast

¹/₂ cup chopped onion

¹/₂ cup canned no-salt-added black
    beans, rinsed and drained

¹/₂ cup canned no-salt-added whole
    kernel corn, rinsed and drained

¹/₂ cup bottled salsa

1   teaspoon ground ancho chile
    pepper

¹/₂ teaspoon dried oregano, crushed

¹/₄ teaspoon ground cumin

¹/₈ teaspoon ground cinnamon

1   4-ounce can diced green chile
    peppers, undrained

1   tablespoon butter

1   tablespoon flour

¹/₂ cup fat-free milk

¹/₄ cup shredded Monterey Jack
    cheese (1 ounce)

Paprika

Fresh cilantro leaves (optional)

PER SERVING: 269 cal., 8 g total fat
(4 g sat. fat), 48 mg chol.,
435 mg sodium, 28 g carb. (4 g fiber,
6 g sugars), 22 g pro. Exchanges:
2 vegetable, 1 starch, 2 lean meat, 1 fat.

1 | Preheat broiler. Remove stems and seeds from poblano chile peppers (see tip, page 17), keeping peppers whole. Place poblano peppers on a foil-lined baking sheet. Broil 3 to 4 inches from the heat for 5 to 6 minutes or until skins are charred and bubbled. Turn poblano peppers over; broil for 5 to 6 minutes more or until skins are charred and bubbled. Bring the foil up around poblano peppers and fold edges together to enclose. Let stand about 15 minutes or until cool enough to handle. Using a sharp knife, loosen edges of skins; gently pull off the skins in strips and discard. Set poblano peppers aside.

2 | Meanwhile, coat an unheated large nonstick skillet with cooking spray; heat skillet over medium heat. Add ground pork and onion; cook until browned, using a wooden spoon to break up meat as it cooks. Drain if needed. Stir black beans, corn, salsa, ancho chile pepper, oregano, cumin, and cinnamon into meat mixture in skillet. Cook about 5 minutes or until heated through. Cover and keep warm.

3 | Preheat oven to 375°F. Coat a 2-quart rectangular baking dish with cooking spray; set aside. For green chile-cheese sauce, place canned green chile peppers in a food processor; cover and process until smooth. Set aside. In a small saucepan melt butter over medium heat. Stir in flour until combined. Stir in milk, whisking until smooth. Cook and stir about 2 minutes or until thickened and bubbly. Stir in pureed green chile peppers and the cheese. Cook and stir until cheese is melted and sauce is smooth.

4 | To stuff poblano peppers, cut each pepper open lengthwise from stem end to tip. Place one of the poblano peppers, open side up, in the prepared baking dish. Spoon about ²/₃ cup of the pork mixture down the center of the pepper. Fold up sides of poblano pepper, leaving some of the filling exposed. Repeat with the remaining poblano peppers and the remaining pork mixture. Pour green chile-cheese sauce over poblano peppers. Cover dish with foil. Bake for 20 to 25 minutes or until heated through. Sprinkle generously with paprika. Let stand for 5 minutes before serving. If desired, garnish with fresh cilantro leaves.

Bruschetta Chicken Breasts

These little chicken bundles are stuffed with a stir-together bruschetta-topping mixture.

 SERVINGS 4 (1 chicken roll and 2 tablespoons sauce each)
CARB. PER SERVING 11 g
PREP 40 minutes
BAKE 25 minutes

Nonstick cooking spray

2 10-ounce skinless, boneless chicken breast halves

3/4 teaspoon dried basil, crushed

2 tablespoons snipped oil-packed dried tomatoes

2 cloves garlic, minced

1/8 teaspoon black pepper

1/3 cup Italian-seasoned dry bread crumbs

1 egg

3/4 cup shredded part-skim mozzarella cheese (3 ounces)

1/2 cup marinara sauce

Snipped fresh basil (optional)

PER SERVING: 304 cal., 10 g total fat (4 g sat. fat), 149 mg chol., 588 mg sodium, 11 g carb. (1 g fiber, 3 g sugars), 39 g pro. Exchanges: 0.5 starch, 5 lean meat, 1 fat.

1 Preheat oven to 375°F. Lightly coat a shallow baking pan with cooking spray; set aside. Trim any remaining fat from the chicken breasts. Halve each chicken breast half. Place each portion between two pieces of plastic wrap. Using the flat side of a meat mallet, pound each chicken piece lightly from center to edge of each portion to make a rectangle about 1/8 inch thick. Remove and discard plastic wrap. Sprinkle 1/4 teaspoon of the dried basil over chicken pieces.

2 In a small bowl stir together the remaining 1/2 teaspoon dried basil, the dried tomatoes, garlic, and pepper. Place bread crumbs in a shallow dish. Place egg in another shallow dish; using a fork, beat egg lightly.

3 Spread a scant tablespoon of the basil mixture on each chicken piece. Place 2 tablespoons of the shredded cheese near an edge of each chicken piece. Fold in sides; starting from the edge with the cheese, roll up jelly-roll style. If necessary, secure with wooden toothpicks.

4 Roll chicken in egg. Dip chicken in bread crumbs, turning to coat evenly. Place rolls, seam sides down, in prepared pan. Bake, uncovered, for 25 to 30 minutes or until an instant-read thermometer inserted into center registers 165°F. Remove toothpicks if necessary. In a small saucepan heat marinara sauce; spoon over chicken rolls. Sprinkle with the remaining 1/4 cup shredded cheese. If desired, garnish with snipped fresh basil.

Creamy Basil-Rosemary Chicken and Rice

Strip the basil and rosemary leaves from the stems into a small glass measuring cup. Then use kitchen scissors to snip the leaves into little pieces.

SERVINGS 4 (1 cup each)
CARB. PER SERVING 21 g
PREP 25 minutes
COOK 30 minutes

1 teaspoon canola oil

1½ cups chopped onions

1 cup thinly sliced celery

1 14.5-ounce can reduced-sodium chicken broth

1 cup instant brown rice

2 cups chopped cooked chicken breast

4 ounces light semisoft cheese with garlic and fine herbs

¼ cup water

1 clove garlic, minced

¼ cup snipped fresh basil

1 tablespoon snipped fresh rosemary

⅛ teaspoon salt

Snipped fresh basil (optional)

Snipped fresh rosemary (optional)

1 In a medium nonstick skillet heat oil over medium-low heat. Add onions; cook about 15 minutes or until golden brown. Stir in celery; cook about 4 minutes more or until celery is tender. Stir in broth and rice. Bring to boiling; reduce heat. Simmer, covered, about 10 minutes or until liquid is absorbed.

2 Stir in chicken, cheese, the water, and garlic; heat through, stirring occasionally. Stir in the ¼ cup basil, the 1 tablespoon rosemary, and the salt. If desired, sprinkle with additional basil and/or rosemary.

PER SERVING: 294 cal., 10 g total fat (5 g sat. fat), 80 mg chol., 559 mg sodium, 21 g carb. (3 g fiber, 4 g sugars), 29 g pro. Exchanges: 1 vegetable, 1 starch, 3.5 lean meat, 0.5 fat.

Tandoori-Spiced Chicken and Rice Bake

Use caution when removing the foil from a hot baking dish. Steam escapes and will burn your hand or arm if you aren't careful.

SERVINGS 4 (1 chicken breast half and 1 cup rice mixture each)
CARB. PER SERVING 35 g
PREP 45 minutes
BAKE 1 hour 5 minutes

Nonstick cooking spray

1 tablespoon butter

1/2 cup coarsely chopped onion (1 medium)

1/2 cup coarsely shredded carrot (1 medium)

1/2 cup chopped red sweet pepper (1 small)

1/2 of a fresh Anaheim chile pepper, seeded and chopped (see tip, page 17)

1 small zucchini, halved lengthwise and cut into 1/4-inch-thick slices

2 cloves garlic, thinly sliced

1 14.5-ounce can reduced-sodium chicken broth

2/3 cup uncooked long grain brown rice

1/2 cup water

1/4 cup no-salt-added tomato paste

1 recipe Tandoori Spice Mixture

1 1/2 teaspoons butter

4 4- to 5-ounce skinless, boneless chicken breast halves

Snipped fresh cilantro

1 Preheat oven to 350°F. Lightly coat a 2-quart rectangular baking dish with cooking spray; set aside.

2 In a large skillet melt the 1 tablespoon butter over medium heat. Add onion, carrot, sweet pepper, and chile pepper; cook and stir for 6 minutes. Stir in zucchini and garlic. Cook and stir for 3 minutes more.

3 Stir in broth, rice, the water, tomato paste, and 1 tablespoon of the Tandoori Spice Mixture. Bring to boiling; boil for 1 minute. Carefully pour rice and vegetable mixture into prepared baking dish. Cover tightly with foil. Bake for 45 minutes.

4 Meanwhile, sprinkle the remaining Tandoori Spice Mixture evenly over all sides of the chicken. Using your fingers, rub spices into the meat. In a large skillet melt the 1 1/2 teaspoons butter over medium-high heat. Cook chicken in hot butter about 4 minutes or just until browned, turning once halfway through cooking. Transfer chicken to plate; chill in refrigerator until needed.

5 Remove rice mixture from oven and uncover it. Arrange chicken pieces on rice mixture. Replace foil. Bake for 20 to 25 minutes more or until chicken is done (165°F) and rice is tender. To serve, sprinkle with cilantro.

TANDOORI SPICE MIXTURE: In a small bowl combine 1 teaspoon mild yellow curry powder, 1 teaspoon garam masala, 1/2 teaspoon ground ginger, 1/2 teaspoon ground cumin, 1/2 teaspoon ground coriander, 1/2 teaspoon ground cardamom, 1/4 teaspoon salt, 1/4 teaspoon ground cinnamon, and 1/8 teaspoon black pepper.

30 grams pro.

PER SERVING: 344 cal., 9 g total fat (4 g sat. fat), 84 mg chol., 575 mg sodium, 35 g carb. (4 g fiber, 6 g sugars), 30 g pro. Exchanges: 1 vegetable, 2 starch, 3.5 lean meat.

Honey Chicken Stir-Fry

Frozen and shelf-stable cooked brown rice are quick options to cooking your own. All you need to do is heat and serve.

SERVINGS 8 (³/₄ cup chicken mixture and ¹/₃ cup rice each)
CARB. PER SERVING 34 g
START TO FINISH 30 minutes

1½ pounds skinless, boneless chicken breast halves, cut into thin bite-size strips

¼ teaspoon salt

¼ teaspoon black pepper

2 teaspoons olive oil

1 16-ounce package frozen stir-fry vegetables with broccoli, thawed and drained

1 recipe Honey Stir-Fry Sauce

2²/₃ cups hot cooked brown rice

¼ cup sliced green onions

³/₄ cup chow mein noodles (optional)

1 | Sprinkle chicken with the salt and pepper. In a large skillet heat oil over medium heat. Add half of the chicken; cook and stir for 3 to 4 minutes or until no longer pink. Remove from skillet. Repeat with the remaining chicken.

2 | Return all of the chicken to skillet. Stir in thawed vegetables and Honey Stir-Fry Sauce. Cook and stir until thickened and bubbly. Cook and stir for 2 minutes more.

3 | Serve chicken mixture over hot rice. Sprinkle with green onions. If desired, serve with chow mein noodles.

HONEY STIR-FRY SAUCE: In a small bowl combine 6 tablespoons honey; ¼ cup reduced-sodium chicken broth; 3 tablespoons reduced-sodium soy sauce; 2 tablespoons cider vinegar; 4 cloves garlic, minced; 1 teaspoon toasted sesame oil; ¼ teaspoon ground ginger; and ⅛ teaspoon cayenne pepper. Stir in 1 tablespoon cornstarch until dissolved.

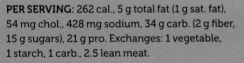

PER SERVING: 262 cal., 5 g total fat (1 g sat. fat), 54 mg chol., 428 mg sodium, 34 g carb. (2 g fiber, 15 g sugars), 21 g pro. Exchanges: 1 vegetable, 1 starch, 1 carb., 2.5 lean meat.

QUICK TIP
To quickly thaw the frozen vegetables, place them in a colander and run cool water over them. Once thawed, drain the vegetables well and use paper towels to blot the water.

Balsamic Chicken with Roasted Orange Asparagus

One orange is all you need—shred the peel and then cut the orange in half. Juice half of the orange and cut the remaing half into wedges.

SERVINGS 4 (1 chicken breast half and 1/4 of the asparagus each)
CARB. PER SERVING 8 g
PREP 25 minutes
COOK 19 minutes
ROAST 12 minutes

- 1 tablespoon snipped fresh rosemary or oregano or 1 teaspoon dried rosemary or oregano, crushed
- 2 cloves garlic, minced
- 1/2 teaspoon salt
- 1/4 teaspoon black pepper
- 4 small bone-in chicken breast halves, skinned (2 pounds total)
- Nonstick cooking spray
- 1/2 cup reduced-sodium chicken broth
- 1/4 cup balsamic vinegar
- 1 pound asparagus, trimmed
- 2 tablespoons orange juice
- 4 orange wedges
- Shredded orange peel

PER SERVING: 207 cal., 4 g total fat (1 g sat. fat), 94 mg chol., 501 mg sodium, 8 g carb. (1 g fiber, 5 g sugars), 33 g pro. Exchanges: 1 vegetable, 4 lean meat.

1 Preheat oven to 425°F. In a small bowl combine rosemary, garlic, 1/4 teaspoon of the salt, and 1/8 teaspoon of the pepper. Sprinkle herb mixture evenly over skinned sides of the chicken breast halves; rub in with your fingers.

2 Coat an unheated very large nonstick skillet with cooking spray. Heat over medium heat. Add chicken pieces, herb sides down. Cook for 4 to 6 minutes or until browned. Turn pieces over. Remove skillet from the heat. Carefully add broth and vinegar to the skillet. Return skillet to heat. Cover and cook for 15 to 20 minutes or until an instant-read thermometer inserted in chicken registers 170°F, spooning broth mixture over chicken occasionally.

3 Meanwhile, in a 15×10×1-inch baking pan arrange asparagus spears in a single layer. Drizzle with orange juice and sprinkle with the remaining 1/4 teaspoon salt and the remaining 1/8 teaspoon pepper.

4 Roast asparagus for 12 to 15 minutes or until crisp-tender. To serve, place one chicken piece on each of four serving plates. Spoon pan juices evenly over chicken pieces. Divide asparagus spears among the plates. Serve with orange wedges and garnish with orange peel.

Chicken Pot Pie

Butter is typically brushed on sheets of phyllo, but here they are coated with nonstick cooking spray. The result—crispy phyllo that is light in calories.

SERVINGS 4 (1 casserole each)
CARB. PER SERVING 34 g
PREP 45 minutes
ROAST 25 minutes
BAKE 15 minutes
STAND 10 minutes

- 1 whole bulb garlic
- 1 tablespoon olive oil
- 2 cups sliced fresh button mushrooms
- 2 medium carrots, cut into $\frac{1}{2}$-inch slices
- 1 medium parsnip, cut into $\frac{1}{2}$-inch slices
- $\frac{1}{2}$ cup chopped onion
- $\frac{1}{2}$ cup reduced-sodium chicken broth
- 1 teaspoon dried thyme, crushed
- $\frac{1}{2}$ teaspoon salt
- $\frac{1}{4}$ teaspoon black pepper
- 2 cups fat-free milk
- 3 tablespoons flour
- 2 cups cubed cooked chicken breast (about 10 ounces)
- 4 sheets frozen phyllo dough (14×9-inch rectangles), thawed

Nonstick cooking spray

Black pepper (optional)

PER SERVING: 308 cal., 6 g total fat (1 g sat. fat), 61 mg chol., 570 mg sodium, 34 g carb. (3 g fiber, 11 g sugars), 31 g pro. Exchanges: 1 vegetable, 2 starch, 3 lean meat.

1 Preheat oven to 425°F. Peel away the dry outer layers of skin from the garlic bulb, leaving skins and cloves intact. Cut off the pointed top portion (about $\frac{1}{4}$ inch), leaving bulb intact but exposing the individual cloves. Place the garlic bulb, cut side up, in a custard cup. Drizzle with about $\frac{1}{2}$ teaspoon of the olive oil. Cover with foil. Roast for 25 to 35 minutes or until the cloves feel soft when pressed. Set aside just until cool enough to handle. Squeeze out the garlic paste from individual cloves.

2 Meanwhile, heat the remaining olive oil in a large skillet. Add mushrooms, carrots, parsnip, and onion. Cook for 10 minutes, stirring occasionally. Add broth, thyme, salt, and $\frac{1}{4}$ teaspoon pepper. Bring to boiling; reduce heat. Simmer, covered, for 5 to 10 minutes or just until vegetables are tender. Stir in garlic paste.

3 In a medium bowl whisk together milk and flour until smooth; add all at once to mushroom mixture. Cook and stir over medium heat until thickened and bubbly. Stir in chicken. Divide mixture evenly among four 12-ounce individual oven-safe dishes. Set aside.

4 Unfold phyllo dough; remove 1 sheet of the phyllo dough and place on a flat surface. (As you work, cover the remaining phyllo dough with plastic wrap to prevent it from drying out.) Lightly coat the phyllo sheet with cooking spray. Lay another sheet of phyllo dough on top of the first sheet and lightly coat with cooking spray. Repeat with the remaining 2 phyllo sheets. Cut phyllo stack in half crosswise. Place one stack on top of the other to make a 9×7-inch stack of 8 sheets.

5 Using a pizza cutter, cut phyllo stack into 16 strips. Place four strips in a woven pattern on top of the chicken mixture in each baking dish.

6 Bake for 15 to 20 minutes or until the filling is bubbly and phyllo is golden brown. Let stand for 10 minutes before serving. If desired, sprinkle tops of pot pies with additional pepper.

Chicken Alfredo

A tangy sour cream sauce takes the place of the traditional high-fat cream sauce. The result is divine.

SERVINGS 6 (^{2}/$_3$ cup pasta mixture and ^{1}/$_2$ cup chicken mixture each)
CARB. PER SERVING 25 g
START TO FINISH 35 minutes

- 4 ounces dried whole grain linguine
- 5 cups bite-size strips zucchini and/or yellow summer squash
- 1 tablespoon butter
- 1 pound skinless, boneless chicken breast halves, cut into bite-size strips
- 1 small onion, cut into thin wedges
- 2 cloves garlic, minced
- 1 8-ounce carton light sour cream
- 2 tablespoons flour
- ^{2}/$_3$ cup fat-free milk
- ^{1}/$_2$ teaspoon salt
- ^{1}/$_8$ teaspoon black pepper
- ^{1}/$_4$ cup finely shredded Parmesan cheese (1 ounce)
- 2 tablespoons snipped fresh parsley
- ^{1}/$_4$ cup finely shredded Parmesan cheese (1 ounce)

PER SERVING: 272 cal., 10 g total fat (6 g sat. fat), 57 mg chol., 477 mg sodium, 25 g carb. (3 g fiber, 5 g sugars), 21 g pro. Exchanges: 1 vegetable, 1.5 starch, 2 lean meat, 1 fat.

1 In a Dutch oven cook linguine according to package directions, adding the zucchini strips for the last 2 minutes of cooking time. Drain well. Return to hot Dutch oven; cover and keep warm.

2 Meanwhile, in a large nonstick skillet melt butter over medium heat. Add chicken, onion, and garlic. Cook about 8 minutes or until chicken is cooked through and onion is tender, stirring occasionally.

3 In a medium bowl stir together sour cream and flour until well mixed. Stir in milk, salt, and pepper. Add sour cream mixture to chicken mixture in skillet. Cook and stir over medium heat just until bubbly; cook and stir for 2 minutes more. Add ^{1}/$_4$ cup Parmesan cheese, stirring until melted.

4 Serve the chicken mixture over the pasta-zucchini mixture. Sprinkle with parsley and ^{1}/$_4$ cup Parmesan cheese.

Lemony Chicken and Green Beans

If you only have plain fine dry bread crumbs, stir in $^1/_4$ teaspoon dried Italian seasoning to create seasoned ones.

SERVINGS 4 (1 chicken breast half and $^3/_4$ cup green bean mixture each)

CARB. PER SERVING 12 g

START TO FINISH 20 minutes

4 skinless, boneless chicken breast halves (about 1$^1/_4$ pounds total)

1 tablespoon Dijon-style mustard

$^1/_4$ teaspoon salt

$^1/_4$ teaspoon black pepper

$^1/_4$ cup seasoned fine dry bread crumbs

2 tablespoons olive oil

2 lemons

8 ounces fresh green beans, trimmed

1 tablespoon capers, rinsed and drained

Lemon wedges (optional)

1 | Place each chicken breast half between two pieces of plastic wrap. Using the flat side of a meat mallet, pound each chicken breast half lightly until an even thickness. Remove and discard plastic wrap. Brush chicken with mustard; sprinkle evenly with the salt and pepper. Sprinkle bread crumbs evenly over all sides of chicken to coat.

2 | In a very large skillet heat half of the oil over medium heat. Add chicken; cook about 8 minutes or until an instant-read thermometer inserted in chicken registers 165°F, turning once halfway through cooking time. Transfer to four dinner plates; keep warm.

3 | Slice 1 lemon and squeeze juice from the other lemon. Add the remaining oil to the skillet. Cook green beans in hot oil about 4 minutes or until crisp-tender, scraping up browned bits. Add the lemon slices, lemon juice, and capers to skillet. Cook and stir for 1 minute. Serve bean mixture with chicken. If desired, serve with lemon wedges.

PER SERVING: 278 cal., 11 g total fat (2 g sat. fat), 91 mg chol., 599 mg sodium, 12 g carb. (3 g fiber, 3 g sugars), 32 g pro. Exchanges: 1 vegetable, 0.5 starch, 4 lean meat, 1 fat.

12 grams carb.

QUICK TIP
If you don't have a flat-sided meat mallet, use a heavy small saucepan to pound the chicken pieces into even thickness.

Mini Turkey Meat Loaves with Walnut-Parsley Gremolata

These little ground turkey loaves boast big veggie flavor with mushrooms, onion, and dried tomatoes.

SERVINGS 4 (1 mini meat loaf with 2 tablespoons gremolata each)
CARB. PER SERVING 10 g
PREP 25 minutes
BAKE 20 minutes

Nonstick cooking spray (optional)

2 egg whites

1½ cups chopped fresh mushrooms

⅓ cup rolled oats

¼ cup finely chopped dried tomatoes (not oil-packed)

¼ cup finely chopped onion

½ teaspoon salt

¼ teaspoon black pepper

8 ounces lean uncooked ground turkey

8 ounces extra-lean uncooked ground turkey breast or lean uncooked ground turkey

⅓ cup snipped fresh Italian (flat-leaf) parsley

¼ cup chopped walnuts, toasted

2 teaspoons walnut oil or olive oil

½ teaspoon finely shredded lemon peel

1 tablespoon lemon juice

⅛ teaspoon salt

PER SERVING: 270 cal., 12 g total fat (2 g sat. fat), 68 mg chol., 479 mg sodium, 10 g carb. (2 g fiber, 3 g sugars), 30 g pro. Exchanges: 0.5 starch, 4 lean meat, 1 fat.

1 Preheat oven to 375°F. Line a 15×10×1-inch baking pan with parchment paper or foil; if using foil, coat with cooking spray. Set pan aside. In a large bowl beat egg whites with a fork. Stir in mushrooms, rolled oats, dried tomatoes, onion, the ½ teaspoon salt, and the pepper. Add ground turkey; mix well.

2 Divide meat mixture into four equal portions. Shape each portion into a 4-inch oval that is about 2½ inches wide in the center. Place in the prepared baking pan, leaving 2 inches between ovals. Bake about 20 minutes or until done (165°F).*

3 Meanwhile, for gremolata, in a small bowl combine parsley, walnuts, oil, lemon peel, lemon juice, and the ⅛ teaspoon salt. To serve, transfer each meat loaf to a serving plate. Top evenly with parsley mixture.

*TEST KITCHEN TIP: The internal color of meat loaf is not a reliable doneness indicator. A turkey loaf cooked to 165°F is safe, regardless of color. To measure the doneness of a meat loaf, insert an instant-read thermometer into the center of loaf.

Shrimp, Scallops, and Pineapple Skewers with Cilantro Aïoli

If you use wooden skewers, soak the skewers in enough water to cover for 30 minutes and drain before using.

SERVINGS 8 (1 skewer each)
CARB. PER SERVING 14 g
PREP 35 minutes
MARINATE 30 minutes
GRILL 5 minutes

1 pound fresh or frozen peeled and deveined large shrimp (tails left on)

1 pound fresh or frozen sea scallops

3 tablespoons lime juice

1 tablespoon vegetable oil or canola oil

1 teaspoon garlic powder

1 teaspoon ground coriander

1 teaspoon sweet paprika

1 teaspoon Asian chili sauce (Sriracha sauce)

½ teaspoon black pepper

6 cloves garlic, minced

1 teaspoon olive oil

½ cup finely snipped fresh cilantro

¼ cup light mayonnaise

¼ cup fat-free sour cream

1 fresh serrano chile pepper or jalapeño chile pepper, stemmed, seeded, and finely chopped*

¾ of a fresh pineapple, peeled, cored, and cut into 1½-inch pieces (about 3 cups)

1 | Thaw shrimp and scallops, if frozen. Rinse shrimp and scallops; pat dry with paper towels.

2 | In a large bowl whisk together 2 tablespoons of the lime juice, the vegetable oil, garlic powder, coriander, paprika, chili sauce, and black pepper. Add shrimp and scallops, tossing gently to coat. Cover and marinate in the refrigerator for 30 minutes.

3 | Meanwhile, for aïoli, in a medium microwave-safe bowl stir together garlic and olive oil. Microwave on 100 percent power (high) for 20 seconds; stir. Microwave for 20 seconds more, being careful not to burn garlic. Stir in cilantro, mayonnaise, sour cream, chile pepper, and the remaining 1 tablespoon lime juice. Cover and chill until serving time.

4 | Using sixteen 12-inch skewers (two skewers for each kabob), place skewers in pairs parallel to one another. Alternately thread shrimp, scallops, and pineapple on the skewer pairs, dividing ingredients evenly among skewer pairs and leaving ¼ inch between pieces. For a charcoal or gas grill, place skewers on a greased grill rack directly over medium heat. Cover and grill for 5 to 8 minutes or until shrimp and scallops are opaque, turning once halfway through grilling time. Serve with the aïoli.

*TEST KITCHEN TIP: Because chile peppers contain volatile oils that can burn your skin and eyes, avoid direct contact with them as much as possible. When working with chile peppers, wear plastic or rubber gloves. If your bare hands do touch the peppers, wash your hands and nails well with soap and warm water.

PER SERVING: 183 cal., 7 g total fat (1 g sat. fat), 88 mg chol., 611 mg sodium, 14 g carb. (1 g fiber, 6 g sugars), 15 g pro. Exchanges: 1 fruit, 2 lean meat, 1 fat.

Asian Stir-Fry with Shrimp

To stir-fry, you need a pan with enough room to keep the food moving as it quickly cooks. A 12-inch skillet or large wok is the perfect choice.

SERVINGS 4 (2 cups each)
CARB. PER SERVING 18 g
START TO FINISH 20 minutes

1 pound fresh or frozen medium shrimp

3 tablespoons water

2 tablespoons hoisin sauce

2 tablespoons reduced-sodium soy sauce

2 teaspoons Asian chili sauce (Sriracha sauce)

2 tablespoons canola oil or olive oil

4 cloves garlic, minced

2 teaspoons grated fresh ginger

3 8-ounce packages refrigerated spaghetti-shape noodle substitute (such as House Foods Tofu Shirataki brand)

1 12-ounce package fresh stir-fry vegetable medley

¼ cup sliced green onions (optional)

½ teaspoon toasted sesame oil

1 Thaw shrimp, if frozen. Peel and devein shrimp, leaving tails intact if desired. Rinse shrimp; pat dry with paper towels. Set aside. Meanwhile, in a small bowl whisk together the water, hoisin sauce, soy sauce, and Asian chili sauce; set aside.

2 In a very large skillet heat 1 tablespoon of the oil over medium-high heat. Add shrimp, garlic, and ginger to hot oil. Stir-fry about 2 minutes or until shrimp are opaque. Remove shrimp from skillet; set aside. Meanwhile, drain and rinse the noodle substitute; pat dry with paper towels.

3 Heat the remaining 1 tablespoon oil in the skillet. Add vegetables to hot oil; stir-fry for 3 to 4 minutes or until crisp-tender. Add noodle substitute and hoisin sauce mixture to vegetables in the skillet; stir to coat. Return shrimp to skillet; toss together until heated through. Divide among four bowls. If desired, sprinkle with sliced green onions. Drizzle with sesame oil. Serve immediately (sauce will thin as it stands).

22 grams pro.

PER SERVING: 246 cal., 10 g total fat (1 g sat. fat), 130 mg chol., 631 mg sodium, 18 g carb. (5 g fiber, 6 g sugars), 22 g pro. Exchanges: 2 vegetable, 0.5 starch, 2.5 lean meat, 1.5 fat.

QUICK TIP
If you can't find packaged fresh stir-fry vegetable medley, use vegetables like asparagus, sweet peppers, onions, and edamame.

Greek Tuna Casserole

The oval-shape gratin dish makes a great baking vessel for casseroles, but any 1½-quart baking dish will do.

SERVINGS 6 (1 cup each)
CARB. PER SERVING 24 g
PREP 20 minutes
ROAST 15 minutes
BAKE 40 minutes

Nonstick cooking spray

⅓ cup dried whole wheat orzo pasta

1 medium eggplant, ends trimmed, cut into 1-inch-thick slices

1 large red sweet pepper, quartered

2 tablespoons olive oil

1½ teaspoons finely shredded lemon peel

2 tablespoons lemon juice

1 clove garlic, minced

4 tablespoons snipped fresh oregano

½ teaspoon salt

¼ teaspoon black pepper

½ cup panko bread crumbs

3 5-ounce cans very-low-sodium tuna (water pack), undrained, large pieces broken up

1 9-ounce package frozen artichoke hearts, thawed and, if needed, quartered

½ cup ripe olives, halved

¼ cup crumbled feta cheese (1 ounce)

PER SERVING: 239 cal., 8 g total fat (2 g sat. fat), 37 mg chol., 436 mg sodium, 24 g carb. (9 g fiber, 5 g sugars), 20 g pro. Exchanges: 1 vegetable, 1 starch, 2 lean meat, 1 fat.

1 | Preheat oven to 425°F. Coat a 1½-quart au gratin dish with cooking spray; set aside. Cook pasta according to package directions. Drain and set aside.

2 | Line a 15×10×1-inch baking pan with foil. Lightly coat both sides of each eggplant slice with cooking spray. Place coated eggplant slices in the prepared baking pan. Add sweet pepper quarters to pan with eggplant slices. Roast, uncovered, for 15 to 20 minutes or until eggplant begins to brown and peppers are just tender. Remove from oven; let cool. Cut eggplant and pepper pieces into ¾-inch cubes. Reduce oven temperature to 350°F.

3 | For lemon dressing, in a small bowl whisk together olive oil, 1 teaspoon of the lemon peel, the lemon juice, and garlic. Whisk in 3 tablespoons of the oregano, the salt, and black pepper; set aside. In another small bowl combine panko, the remaining 1 tablespoon oregano, and the remaining ½ teaspoon lemon peel; set aside.

4 | In a large bowl combine cooked orzo, eggplant, sweet pepper, tuna, artichoke hearts, olives, and feta cheese. Stir in the lemon dressing. Spoon mixture into the prepared baking dish. Cover with foil. Bake for 35 to 40 minutes or until heated through. Sprinkle panko mixture over top. Bake, uncovered, for 5 to 8 minutes more or until panko mixture is golden brown.

Flax-Crusted Tuna Burgers with Avocado Aïoli

If you don't have a potato masher, put the aïoli ingredients in a resealable plastic bag, seal, and use your hands to mash the mixture.

SERVINGS 4 (1 tuna patty, $^1/_2$ of a sandwich thin, and about $2^1/_2$ tablespoons aïoli each)
CARB. PER SERVING 23 g
PREP 20 minutes
COOK 10 minutes

1 pound fresh or frozen skinless tuna fillets

1 egg white

$^1/_4$ cup dry whole wheat bread crumbs

1 tablespoon snipped fresh tarragon

$^1/_4$ teaspoon salt

$^1/_8$ teaspoon black pepper

3 tablespoons flaxseed meal

1 tablespoon flaxseeds

Nonstick cooking spray

1 medium avocado, halved, seeded, and peeled

2 tablespoons light mayonnaise

$^1/_2$ teaspoon finely shredded lemon peel

1 tablespoon lemon juice

1 clove garlic, minced

$^1/_8$ teaspoon salt

$^1/_8$ teaspoon black pepper

2 whole grain or whole wheat sandwich thins, split and toasted

1 cup fresh spinach leaves

4 slices tomato

1 | Thaw tuna, if frozen. Rinse tuna; pat dry with paper towels. Finely chop tuna and set aside. In a medium bowl beat egg white with a fork. Stir in bread crumbs, tarragon, the $^1/_4$ teaspoon salt, and $^1/_8$ teaspoon pepper. Add tuna; stir gently to combine. Shape mixture into four $^1/_2$-inch-thick patties, using damp hands if necessary.

2 | In a shallow dish combine the flaxseed meal and flaxseeds. Dip tuna patties into flaxseed mixture, turning to coat evenly.

3 | Coat an unheated large nonstick skillet or nonstick griddle with cooking spray. Heat over medium heat. Add tuna patties; cook for 10 to 12 minutes or until an instant-read thermometer inserted into sides of patties registers 160°F, turning once halfway through cooking time.

4 | Meanwhile, for aïoli, in a medium bowl use a potato masher or fork to coarsely mash avocado. Add mayonnaise, lemon peel, lemon juice, garlic, the $^1/_8$ teaspoon salt, and $^1/_8$ teaspoon pepper. Continue to mash until mixture is well mixed but still slightly chunky.

5 | To serve, place one sandwich thin half, cut side up, on each of four serving plates. Top with spinach leaves and tomato slices. Top each with a cooked tuna patty. Spoon one-fourth of the avocado mixture over each patty.

PER SERVING: 332 cal., 12 g total fat (1 g sat. fat), 47 mg chol., 531 mg sodium, 23 g carb. (8 g fiber, 3 g sugars), 35 g pro. Exchanges: 1 vegetable, 1 starch, 4 lean meat, 1 fat.

QUICK TIP
For a main-dish salad, serve this grilled fish topped with fruit salsa on a bed of mixed salad greens or baby spinach leaves.

Caramelized Salmon with Citrus Salsa

Measure the thickness of the fish before you place it on the grill rack. It will take 7 to 9 minutes to cook per $^1/_2$-inch thickness of fish.

SERVINGS 6 (1 salmon fillet and about $^1/_3$ cup salsa each)
CARB. PER SERVING 13 g
PREP 30 minutes
MARINATE 8 hours
GRILL 7 minutes

6 4-ounce fresh or frozen salmon fillets with skin, about 1 inch thick

2 tablespoons sugar*

$2^1/_2$ teaspoons finely shredded orange peel

1 teaspoon salt

$^1/_4$ teaspoon freshly ground black pepper

2 oranges, peeled, sectioned, and chopped

1 cup chopped fresh pineapple or canned crushed pineapple (juice pack), drained

2 tablespoons snipped fresh cilantro

1 tablespoon finely chopped shallot

2 teaspoons finely chopped fresh jalapeño chile pepper (see tip, *page 35)*

Orange slices (optional)

PER SERVING: 213 cal., 7 g total fat (1 g sat. fat), 62 mg chol., 439 mg sodium, 13 g carb. (1.65 g fiber, 11 g sugars), 23 g pro. Exchanges: 0.5 fruit, 0.5 carb., 3 lean meat, 0.5 fat.

1 Thaw fish, if frozen. In a small bowl stir together sugar, $1^1/_2$ teaspoons of the orange peel, the salt, and black pepper. Sprinkle sugar mixture evenly over salmon (not on skin sides); rub in with your fingers. Place salmon fillets, sugared sides up, in a glass baking dish. Cover dish and refrigerate for at least 8 hours or up to 24 hours.

2 For the citrus salsa, in a small bowl combine the remaining 1 teaspoon orange peel, the chopped oranges, pineapple, cilantro, shallot, and chile pepper. Cover; chill for up to 24 hours.

3 Lift fillets from dish; discard liquid in dish. For a charcoal grill, arrange medium-hot coals around a drip pan. Test for medium heat above the pan. Place fish, skin sides down, on the oiled grill rack over the drip pan. Cover and grill for 7 to 9 minutes per $^1/_2$-inch thickness of fish or until fish flakes easily when tested with a fork. (For a gas grill, preheat grill. Reduce heat to medium. Adjust for indirect cooking. Place fillets on oiled rack over burner that is off. Grill as directed.)

4 To serve, carefully slip a metal spatula between fish and skin, lifting fish up and away from skin. Serve with the citrus salsa. If desired, garnish with orange slices.

*TEST KITCHEN TIP: We do not recommend using a sugar substitute for this recipe.

Crispy Almond Fish with Potato Crisps

For two-color potato crisps, use half of a white-flesh potao and half of a yellow-flesh potato or sweet potato.

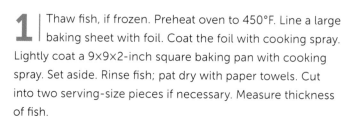

SERVINGS 2 (4 ounces fish and ¹/₂ of a potato each)
CARB. PER SERVING 25 g
PREP 30 minutes
BAKE 15 minutes

8 ounces fresh or frozen skinless cod fillets

Nonstick cooking spray

1 medium white- or yellow-flesh potato or sweet potato (5 to 6 ounces), cut crosswise into ¹/₈-inch-thick slices

¹/₈ teaspoon garlic salt

2 tablespoons flour

1 egg white, lightly beaten

1 tablespoon fat-free milk

2 tablespoons fine dry bread crumbs

2 tablespoons finely chopped almonds

¹/₂ teaspoon snipped fresh thyme

1 tablespoon canola oil

1 Thaw fish, if frozen. Preheat oven to 450°F. Line a large baking sheet with foil. Coat the foil with cooking spray. Lightly coat a 9×9×2-inch square baking pan with cooking spray. Set aside. Rinse fish; pat dry with paper towels. Cut into two serving-size pieces if necessary. Measure thickness of fish.

2 For potato crisps, arrange the potato slices in a single layer on the prepared baking sheet. Coat potato slices with cooking spray. Sprinkle with garlic salt.

3 Bake potato slices for 15 to 20 minutes or until the potatoes are browned and crisp. (If any slices brown more quickly than others, remove from baking sheet and keep warm.)

4 Meanwhile, place flour in a shallow dish. In a second shallow dish whisk together egg white and milk. In a third shallow dish combine bread crumbs, almonds, and thyme. Coat all sides of fillets with flour. Dip fillets into egg mixture and then into bread crumb mixture, turning to coat all sides.

5 Place fish in the prepared baking pan. Drizzle with oil. Bake for 4 to 6 minutes per ¹/₂-inch thickness of fish or until fish begins to flake easily when tested with a fork. Serve fish with potato crisps.

PER SERVING: 307 cal., 11 g total fat (1 g sat. fat), 49 mg chol., 206 mg sodium, 25 g carb. (3 g fiber, 2 g sugars), 27 g pro. Exchanges: 1.5 starch, 3.5 lean meat, 0.5 fat.

Three-Cheese Vegetable Pasta Toss

Try any shape of whole wheat pasta in this quick-to-fix family-style dinner. Add steamed green beans or a fresh green salad to complete the meal.

SERVINGS 5 (1¼ cups pasta mixture each)
CARB. PER SERVING 35 g
START TO FINISH 20 minutes

4 ounces dried whole wheat elbow macaroni (about 1 cup)

⅓ cup part-skim ricotta cheese

2 tablespoons grated Parmesan cheese

½ teaspoon coarse salt

½ teaspoon dried Italian seasoning

⅛ to ¼ teaspoon crushed red pepper

⅛ teaspoon black pepper

1 teaspoon olive oil

1 8-ounce package sliced fresh mushrooms

1 10-ounce package prewashed fresh baby spinach

1 23.5-ounce jar no-salt-added traditional pasta sauce

½ cup shredded part-skim mozzarella cheese (2 ounces)

1 In a large pot bring 4 cups water to boiling. Add macaroni; cook according to package directions. Drain well and return to pasta pot. Meanwhile, in a small bowl stir together ricotta cheese, Parmesan cheese, salt, Italian seasoning, crushed red pepper, and black pepper. Set aside.

2 In a very large nonstick skillet heat oil over medium heat. Add mushrooms; cook about 5 minutes or until tender. Add spinach. Cook and toss until spinach is wilted and liquid is evaporated. Drain well if needed.

3 Stir cheese mixture into hot pasta. Stir in pasta sauce; cook until bubbly. Stir in mushroom-spinach mixture. Sprinkle with mozzarella cheese.

PER SERVING: 254 cal., 9 g total fat (3 g sat. fat), 14 mg chol., 433 mg sodium, 35 g carb. (6 g fiber, 8 g sugars), 14 g pro. Exchanges: 1 vegetable, 2 starch, 1.5 lean meat.

Farro White Bean Cups

Turn this handheld food into a salad by tearing the lettuce leaves into pieces and tossing them together with the bean mixture.

SERVINGS 4 (1 cup bean mixture and 2 lettuce leaves each)
CARB. PER SERVING 36 g
START TO FINISH 25 minutes

- 1 15-ounce can cannellini beans (white kidney beans), rinsed and drained
- 1 cup packaged cooked plain farro, such as Archer Farms Brand, or packaged cooked whole grain brown rice
- ½ cup carrot cut into matchstick-size strips
- ¼ cup coarsely chopped salted dry-roasted pistachio nuts
- 3 tablespoons oil-packed dried tomatoes, drained and chopped
- 3 tablespoons chopped red onion
- 1 avocado, halved, seeded, and peeled
- 2 tablespoons lime juice
- 1 teaspoon olive oil
- 1 clove garlic, minced
- ¼ teaspoon salt
- ¼ teaspoon dried Italian seasoning, crushed
- 8 large butterhead (Boston or Bibb) lettuce leaves or 4 small red sweet peppers, halved lengthwise

PER SERVING: 277 cal., 11 g total fat (1 g sat. fat), 0 mg chol., 463 mg sodium, 36 g carb. (10 g fiber, 2 g sugars), 10 g pro. Exchanges: 1 vegetable, 2 starch, 1 lean meat, 1.5 fat.

1 In a medium bowl combine cannellini beans, farro, carrot, pistachio nuts, tomatoes, and red onion. Cube the avocado and toss with the lime juice. Add the avocado to the bean mixture; toss gently.

2 In a small bowl whisk together oil, garlic, salt, and Italian seasoning. Drizzle over bean mixture. Toss gently to combine.

3 Spoon about ½ cup of the bean mixture into each lettuce leaf or sweet pepper half and place two filled leaves or two pepper halves on each serving plate.

Two-Bean Enchilada Casserole

Use a large spoon to serve this layered favorite or cut it into six rectangles and remove each with a metal spatula or pancake turner.

SERVINGS 6 (1 cup casserole each)
CARB. PER SERVING 38 g
PREP 25 minutes
BAKE 45 minutes

- 1 tablespoon butter
- 1 tablespoon flour
- 1 8-ounce can no-salt-added tomato sauce
- ¾ cup reduced-sodium chicken broth
- 1 tablespoon chili powder
- 1 teaspoon ground cumin
- 1 teaspoon dried oregano, crushed
- ⅛ teaspoon ground cinnamon
- 1 15-ounce can no-salt-added black beans, rinsed and drained
- 1 15-ounce can no-salt-added pinto beans, rinsed and drained
- ¾ cup chopped green sweet pepper
- ½ cup chopped onion
- 1 4-ounce can diced green chile peppers, undrained
- Nonstick cooking spray
- 9 6-inch corn tortillas, cut into wedges
- 2 cups shredded reduced-fat cheddar cheese (8 ounces)
- Chopped fresh tomato (optional)

1 | Preheat oven to 350°F. In a small saucepan melt butter over medium heat. Add flour, stirring until smooth. Stir in tomato sauce, broth, chili powder, cumin, oregano, and cinnamon. Cook and stir until thickened and bubbly. Cook and stir for 1 minute more; set aside.

2 | In a medium bowl combine black beans, pinto beans, sweet pepper, onion, and chile peppers; set aside.

3 | Coat a 2-quart rectangular baking dish with cooking spray. Spread ⅓ cup of the tomato sauce mixture on the bottom of the prepared baking dish. Layer one-third of the tortillas on top of the sauce. Top with one-third of the bean mixture. Spread one-third of the remaining sauce over all. Sprinkle with ⅔ cup of the cheese. Repeat layers twice, starting with tortillas and setting aside the final ⅔ cup cheese.

4 | Cover with foil. Bake for 35 minutes. Uncover and sprinkle with the reserved ⅔ cup cheese. Bake, uncovered, about 10 minutes more or until cheese melts. If desired, top with chopped tomato.

PER SERVING: 323 cal., 11 g total fat (7 g sat. fat), 32 mg chol., 433 mg sodium, 38 g carb. (10 g fiber, 5 g sugars), 19 g pro. Exchanges: 1 vegetable, 2 starch, 2 lean meat, 1 fat.

fresh
salad meals

When it comes to healthful eating, a salad loaded with nutrient-

packed ingredients is sure to fit your meal plan. Easy to make

and colorful to look at, these complete salads meals boast fresh

flavors bite after bite.

Steak and Cabbage Salad with Horseradish Vinaigrette

Horseradish and dill in the dressing add zing to the crunchy vegetable combo. Make this when the garden is exploding with fresh goodness.

SERVINGS 6 (1 cup salad and 2 ounces steak each)
CARB. PER SERVING 8 g
PREP 15 minutes
GRILL 12 minutes
STAND 10 minutes

1   pound beef flank steak

2   tablespoons olive oil

2   tablespoons red wine vinegar

2   tablespoons snipped fresh dill weed

1   tablespoon prepared horseradish

1   teaspoon Dijon-style mustard

½   teaspoon black pepper

¼   teaspoon salt

4   cups coarsely chopped green cabbage

1   medium English cucumber, halved lengthwise and thinly sliced (2 cups)

1   large yellow sweet pepper, cut into bite-size strips

1   large red sweet pepper, cut into bite-size strips

1 Trim fat from steak. For a gas or charcoal grill, place steak on the grill rack directly over medium heat. Cover and grill to desired doneness, turning once halfway through grilling. Allow 12 to 14 minutes for medium rare (145°F) or 15 to 17 minutes for medium (160°F). Transfer steak to a cutting board; cover with foil. Let stand for 10 minutes.

2 For vinaigrette, in a screw-top jar combine olive oil, vinegar, 1 tablespoon of the dill weed, the horseradish, mustard, pepper, and salt. Cover and shake well to combine.

3 In a large bowl combine cabbage, cucumber, and sweet peppers. Drizzle with half the vinaigrette; toss to coat. Transfer to a serving platter or divide evenly among four serving plates. Thinly slice steak. Arrange steak on cabbage mixture. Sprinkle with the remaining 1 tablespoon dill weed and drizzle with the remaining vinaigrette.

PER SERVING: 202 cal., 11 g total fat (3 g sat. fat), 35 mg chol., 186 mg sodium, 8 g carb. (2 g fiber, 4 g sugars), 18 g pro. Exchanges: 1.5 vegetable, 2 lean meat, 1.5 fat.

8 grams carb.

Gingered Beef and Broccoli Salad Bowl

This fresh and flavorful bowl is all about convenience. Choose a bottled ginger vinaigrette or other light Asian-inspired salad dressing.

SERVINGS 4 (2¹/₂ cups each)
CARB. PER SERVING 13 g
START TO FINISH 20 minutes

- 12 ounces boneless beef sirloin steak
- ²/₃ cup bottled light ginger vinaigrette salad dressing
- 3 cups broccoli florets
- 8 cups mixed spring salad greens or baby salad greens
- 1 medium red sweet pepper, cut into bite-size strips

QUICK TIP
Look for broccoli florets and cut-up sweet pepper in the produce or deli section of your supermarket.

PER SERVING: 240 cal., 10 g total fat (2 g sat. fat), 59 mg chol., 504 mg sodium, 13 g carb. (1 g fiber, 9 g sugars), 23 g pro. Exchanges: 2 vegetable, 3 lean meat, 1 fat.

1 Trim fat from beef; thinly slice beef across the grain into bite-size strips. Set aside.

2 In a wok or large skillet heat 2 tablespoons of the salad dressing over medium-high heat. Add broccoli. Cook and stir for 3 minutes. Add beef to wok. Cook and stir for 2 to 3 minutes more or until meat is slightly pink in center. Remove beef and broccoli from wok.

3 In a large bowl toss together beef, broccoli, salad greens, and sweet pepper. Drizzle with the remaining salad dressing; toss to coat.

Citrus Pork and Arugula Salad

When in peak season, use two medium fresh apricots, halved, seeded, and quartered, in place of the canned apricots.

>> SERVINGS 4 (1½ cups arugula, 2½ to 3 ounces cooked meat, and 2 tablespoons dressing each)
CARB. PER SERVING 19 g
START TO FINISH 30 minutes

- 1 1-pound pork tenderloin
- ¼ teaspoon salt
- ¼ teaspoon black pepper
- 1 tablespoon canola oil
- ½ teaspoon finely shredded orange peel
- ⅓ cup orange juice
- 1 tablespoon rice vinegar or white wine vinegar
- 2 teaspoons reduced-sodium soy sauce
- 2 teaspoons honey
- 1 teaspoon toasted sesame oil
- ½ teaspoon grated fresh ginger or ⅛ teaspoon ground ginger
- 6 cups baby arugula
- ½ cup canned unpeeled apricot halves in light syrup,* drained and quartered
- 1 small avocado, peeled, seeded, and sliced or chopped
- ¼ cup dried apricots, sliced

1 Trim fat from pork. Cut pork crosswise into ¼-inch slices. Sprinkle with the salt and pepper.

2 In a very large skillet cook pork, half at a time, in hot oil over medium-high heat for 2 to 3 minutes or until meat is just slightly pink in center, turning once. Remove from skillet and set aside.

3 For dressing, in a screw-top jar combine orange peel and juice, vinegar, soy sauce, honey, sesame oil, and ginger. Cover and shake well to combine.

4 Place arugula on a serving platter. Top with pork slices, canned apricots, avocado slices, and dried apricots. Drizzle with the dressing.

PER SERVING: 272 cal., 11 g total fat (2 g sat. fat), 74 mg chol., 314 mg sodium, 19 g carb. (3 g fiber, 15 g sugars), 26 g pro. Exchanges: 2 vegetable, 0.5 fruit, 3 lean meat, 1 fat.

Pork, Sweet Potato, and Apple Salad with Greens

Mustard greens add a peppery bite to this colorful salad. If you can't find them, the more-popular kale is tasty, too.

SERVINGS 4 (2 cups each)
CARB. PER SERVING 27 g
PREP 20 minutes
COOK 13 minutes

2 tablespoons white balsamic vinegar or white wine vinegar

2 tablespoons olive oil

2 teaspoons Dijon-style mustard

1 teaspoon honey

½ teaspoon bottled hot pepper sauce

¼ teaspoon salt

¼ teaspoon black pepper

1 pound sweet potatoes, peeled and cut into ½-inch cubes

Nonstick cooking spray

1 pound all-natural pork tenderloin, trimmed and cut into 1-inch cubes

4 cups torn mustard greens or kale (4 ounces)

1 large apple (such as Gala), thinly sliced (1 cup)

1 For dressing, in a screw-top jar combine vinegar, olive oil, mustard, honey, hot pepper sauce, salt, and pepper. Cover and shake well to combine. Set aside.

2 Place sweet potatoes in a steamer basket; set over boiling water. Cover and steam sweet potatoes about 7 minutes or until tender. Transfer potatoes to a large bowl. Drizzle with 1 tablespoon of the dressing. Toss gently to coat; set aside.

3 Coat an unheated large nonstick skillet with cooking spray. Add pork; cook and stir about 6 minutes or until pork is browned but still slightly pink in the center. Remove from heat. Add pork, mustard greens, and apple to the sweet potatoes. Shake remaining dressing; pour over sweet potato mixture. Toss to coat. Serve warm.

9 grams fat

PER SERVING: 294 cal., 9 g total fat (2 g sat. fat), 73 mg chol., 304 mg sodium, 27 g carb. (4 g fiber, 12 g sugars), 26 g pro. Exchanges: 0.5 vegetable, 1 starch, 0.5 carb., 3.5 lean meat, 0.5 fat.

QUICK TIP
Tossing the warm sweet potatoes with a little dressing lets them soak up the flavor.

BBQ Chicken and Roasted Corn Salad

Pounding the chicken to an even thickness allows it to cook quickly and evenly under the broiler.

SERVINGS 4 (1³/₄ cups salad, 4 ounces chicken, and about 1 tablespoon dressing each)
CARB. PER SERVING 30 g
PREP 25 minutes
BROIL 6 minutes

- 1 to 1¼ pounds skinless, boneless chicken breast halves
- 2 teaspoons ground ancho chile pepper or chili powder
- 1 teaspoon dried oregano, crushed
- 1 teaspoon dried thyme, crushed
- ¼ teaspoon salt
- ¼ teaspoon black pepper
- 1 15-ounce can no-salt-added black beans, rinsed and drained
- 1 cup frozen whole kernel corn, thawed
- 1 tablespoon canola oil
- 2 tablespoons bottled light ranch salad dressing
- 2 tablespoons low-sodium barbecue sauce
- 1 tablespoon white wine vinegar
- 4 cups chopped romaine lettuce
- 1 cup cherry tomatoes, halved
- 1 ounce queso fresco, crumbled, or Monterey Jack cheese, shredded (¼ cup)

PER SERVING: 345 cal., 11 g total fat (2 g sat. fat), 80 mg chol., 435 mg sodium, 30 g carb. (8 g fiber, 5 g sugars), 33 g pro. Exchanges: 1.5 vegetable, 1 starch, 0.5 carb., 0.5 fat.

1 Place each chicken breast half between two pieces of plastic wrap. Using the flat side of a meat mallet, pound chicken to about ½-inch thickness. Remove plastic wrap.

2 Preheat broiler. In a small bowl stir together ground chile pepper, oregano, thyme, salt, and black pepper. Sprinkle half of the spice mixture evenly over chicken pieces; rub in with your fingers.

3 In a medium bowl combine beans, corn, oil, and the remaining half of the spice mixture. Stir to combine.

4 Line a 15x10x1-inch baking pan with foil. Place chicken on one side of the pan. Add bean mixture to the other side of the pan. Broil 4 to 5 inches from the heat for 6 to 8 minutes or until chicken is tender and an instant-read thermometer inserted in chicken registers 165°F, turning chicken and stirring bean mixture once halfway through broiling.

5 Meanwhile, in a small bowl combine salad dressing, barbecue sauce, and vinegar; set aside.

6 To assemble, divide romaine among four serving plates. Slice chicken. Top romaine with bean mixture, chicken, and tomatoes, dividing evenly. Sprinkle with queso fresco and serve with salad dressing mixture.

Picadillo-Style Chicken Taco Salad

Picadillo refers to a sweet and tangy Cuban-style dish that contains pimiento-stuffed green olives and raisins. Here dried plums stand in for the raisins.

SERVINGS 4 (1$^1/_2$ cups greens, $^1/_4$ of the chicken mixture, 1 tablespoon cheese, and $^1/_2$ tostada shell each)
CARB. PER SERVING 25 g
START TO FINISH 30 minutes

12 ounces uncooked ground chicken

$^1/_3$ cup chopped onion

2 teaspoons ground coriander

2 teaspoons ground cumin

$^1/_2$ teaspoon salt

1 14.5-ounce can no-salt-added diced tomatoes, undrained

$^2/_3$ cup finely chopped, peeled potato (1 small)

$^1/_4$ cup snipped pitted dried plums (prunes)

$^1/_4$ cup chopped pimiento-stuffed green olives

2 corn tostada shells

6 cups shredded romaine lettuce

$^1/_4$ cup shredded reduced-fat Monterey Jack cheese (1 ounce)

Sliced green onion (optional)

Snipped fresh cilantro (optional)

1 In a large skillet cook chicken and chopped onion over medium heat until chicken is no longer pink, using a wooden spoon to break up chicken as it cooks. Drain off fat. Add coriander, cumin, and salt to chicken mixture in skillet; cook and stir for 1 to 2 minutes. Add tomatoes, potato, dried plums, and olives. Bring to boiling; reduce heat. Simmer, covered, about 10 minutes or until potatoes are tender. Uncover; cook about 3 minutes more or until most of the liquid has evaporated.

2 Meanwhile, heat tostada shells according to package directions until crisp. Arrange shredded romaine on a serving platter. Spoon chicken mixture over romaine. Sprinkle cheese over all. Coarsely crush the tostada shells; sprinkle over salad. If desired, garnish with green onion and/or cilantro.

PER SERVING: 272 cal., 12 g total fat (4 g sat. fat), 78 mg chol., 596 mg sodium, 25 g carb. (5 g fiber, 9 g sugars), 20 g pro. Exchanges: 2 vegetable, 0.5 fruit, 0.5 starch, 2 lean meat, 1 fat.

"Fried" Chicken Salad

Use high-quality frozen chicken pieces to save all kinds of time when making this satisfying salad.

SERVINGS 1
CARB. PER SERVING 35 g
START TO FINISH 15 minutes

- 3 ounces lightly breaded chicken chunks, such as Perdue Simply Smart brand
- 1 tablespoon white balsamic vinegar
- 1 teaspoon olive oil
- 1 teaspoon honey mustard
- 1 teaspoon honey
- 1/8 teaspoon black pepper
- 2 to 3 cups packaged chopped romaine lettuce
- 6 cherry tomatos, halved (3 ounces)
- 1/4 cup whole grain large-cut croutons, such as Marzetti brand, coarsely crushed

1 Microwave chicken chunks according to package directions.

2 For dressing, in a small bowl whisk together vinegar, oil, honey mustard, honey, and pepper; set aside.

3 In a bowl combine romaine, tomatoes, and hot cooked chicken. Drizzle dressing over salad. Sprinkle with croutons.

PER SERVING: 346 cal., 13 g total fat (2 g sat. fat), 40 mg chol., 593 mg sodium, 35 g carb. (5 g fiber, 17 g sugars), 21 g pro. Exchanges: 1 starch, 1 carb., 3 lean meat, 1.5 fat.

QUICK TIP

For this salad and other green salads, turn to bagged chopped romaine or other salad greens to shave a few minutes off the prep time.

Orange Cranberry Club Salad

For no turkey leftovers, use smaller turkey breast tenderloins and adjust the roasting time.

SERVINGS 4 (1¾ cups salad, 2½ ounces turkey, and 2 tablespoons dressing each)
CARB. PER SERVING 15 g
PREP 30 minutes
ROAST 1 hour 15 minutes
STAND 15 minutes

¼ cup low-sugar orange marmalade

2 tablespoons Dijon-style mustard

1 2½-pound turkey breast half with bone

2 slices turkey bacon

2 tablespoons cider vinegar

2 tablespoons olive oil

2 tablespoons low-sugar orange marmalade

1½ teaspoons Dijon-style mustard

2 tablespoons snipped dried cranberries

1 to 2 tablespoons orange juice

6 cups chopped romaine lettuce

1 cup chopped tomato

¼ cup shredded reduced-fat cheddar cheese (1 ounce)

2 tablespoons shredded Swiss cheese

2 tablespoons low-sodium or unsalted croutons

PER SERVING: 310 cal., 12 g total fat (3 g sat. fat), 84 mg chol., 370 mg sodium, 15 g carb. (2 g fiber, 10 g sugars), 33 g pro. Exchanges: 1 starch, 4 lean meat, 1 fat.

1 Preheat oven to 325°F. In a small bowl stir together the ¼ cup marmalade and 2 tablespoons mustard; set aside. Remove skin from turkey breast. Insert an oven-going meat thermometer into the center of the turkey breast. The tip should not touch bone.

2 Place turkey breast, bone side down, on a rack in a shallow roasting pan. Roast, uncovered, for 1¼ to 1½ hours or until juices run clear and turkey is no longer pink (170°F), brushing occasionally with marmalade mixture during the last 15 minutes of roasting. Remove turkey from oven; cover with foil. Let stand for 15 minutes before slicing.

3 Meanwhile, cook turkey bacon according to package directions. Drain on paper towels. Coarsely chop bacon.

4 For dressing, in a small bowl whisk together vinegar, olive oil, 2 tablespoons orange marmalade, and 1½ teaspoons mustard. Stir in the dried cranberries and enough orange juice to reach desired consistency.

5 Coarsely shred half of the turkey for the salad. Cover and chill remaining half of the turkey and save for another use.

6 To serve, arrange romaine on a large serving platter. Top with turkey, tomato, turkey bacon, cheddar cheese, Swiss cheese, and croutons.

Teriyaki Shrimp and Edamame Salad

Edamame (sweet soybeans) not only packs protein and fiber into this salad, it contributes an irresistible chewy texture and bright color.

SERVINGS 4 (2^1/3 cups each)
CARB. PER SERVING 15 g
START TO FINISH 25 minutes

½ cup frozen sweet soybeans (edamame)

2 ounces dried rotini or radiatore pasta

3 cups packaged fresh baby spinach

2 cups shredded romaine lettuce

¾ cup coarsely shredded carrots

¾ cup fresh pea pods, trimmed, strings removed, and halved

1 small yellow or red sweet pepper, cut into thin strips

¼ cup thinly sliced green onions

6 ounces cooked medium shrimp, halved horizontally

3 tablespoons rice vinegar or cider vinegar

1 tablespoon canola oil

1 tablespoon reduced-sodium soy sauce

4 cloves garlic, minced

1 teaspoon toasted sesame oil

1 teaspoon grated fresh ginger

⅛ teaspoon crushed red pepper

1 Cook soybeans according to package directions; drain. Cook pasta according to package directions; drain and rinse with cold water.

2 Divide spinach and romaine among four shallow bowls. Top each with carrots, pea pods, sweet pepper, sweet soybeans, and green onions. In a medium bowl combine shrimp and cooked pasta; set aside.

3 For dressing, in a screw-top jar combine vinegar, canola oil, soy sauce, garlic, toasted sesame oil, ginger, and crushed red pepper. Cover and shake well to combine. Pour half of the dressing mixture over the shrimp and pasta; toss to coat.

4 Top salad mixture in each bowl with shrimp mixture. Drizzle salads with remaining dressing mixture.

PER SERVING: 181 cal., 7 g total fat (1 g sat. fat), 90 mg chol., 593 mg sodium, 15 g carb. (4 g fiber, 3 g sugars), 15 g pro. Exchanges: 1.5 vegetable, 0.5 starch, 1.5 lean meat, 1 fat.

QUICK TIP
For even faster preparation, use ^{1}/3 cup bottled light ginger vinaigrette salad dressing and skip making your own in Step 3.

Tuna-Nectarine Salad with Bread Toasts

Greek yogurt and buttermilk give the dressing for this salad tang and body without adding sodium.

SERVINGS 4 (1¹/₄ cups salad, 1 tablespoon pecans, ¹/₂ of a sandwich thin each)
CARB. PER SERVING 28 g
START TO FINISH 25 minutes

- ¹/₂ cup plain fat-free Greek yogurt
- 3 tablespoons low-fat buttermilk
- 2 tablespoons mayonnaise
- ¹/₄ teaspoon garlic powder
- 2 tablespoons snipped fresh chives
- 1 11-ounce pouch chunk light tuna in water, drained
- 4 ripe, yet firm, nectarines or peaches, pitted and diced
- ¹/₄ cup chopped pecans, toasted
- 2 whole wheat sandwich thins, split, toasted, and quartered

1 In a bowl whisk together yogurt, buttermilk, mayonnaise, and garlic powder until smooth. Stir in chives.

2 Add tuna and nectarines to the yogurt mixture; toss gently to mix. Spoon tuna salad onto four serving plates; sprinkle with pecans. Serve with toasted bread.

PER SERVING: 319 cal., 12 g total fat (2 g sat. fat), 27 mg chol., 441 mg sodium, 28 g carb. (6 g fiber, 14 g sugars), 28 g pro. Exchanges: 1 fruit, 1 starch, 3 lean meat, 1 fat.

Bulgur-Mango Salad

Traditional tabbouleh becomes a hearty meal with the addition of garbanzo beans, mango, and feta.

SERVINGS 5 (1 cup bulgur mixture and 1 cup greens each)
CARB. PER SERVING 36 g
PREP 20 minutes
STAND 1 hour

- 3 cups boiling water
- 1/2 cup uncooked bulgur
- 1 15-ounce can reduced-sodium garbanzo beans (chickpeas), rinsed and drained
- 1 1/2 cups chopped fresh or frozen mango
- 1/2 cup chopped red onion
- 1/3 cup lime juice
- 2 tablespoons canola oil
- 1/2 teaspoon ground cinnamon
- 1/4 teaspoon salt
- 1/4 teaspoon ground cumin
- 1/8 teaspoon cayenne pepper
- 3 tablespoons snipped fresh mint
- 5 cups mixed spring salad greens
- 4 ounces feta cheese, crumbled
- Snipped fresh mint (optional)

PER SERVING: 274 cal., 12 g total fat (4 g sat. fat), 20 mg chol., 544 mg sodium, 36 g carb. (8 g fiber, 9 g sugars), 10 g pro. Exchanges: 0.5 fruit, 1.5 starch, 1 medium-fat meat, 1 fat.

1 | In a medium bowl pour boiling water over bulgur; cover with plastic wrap. Let stand at room temperature for 1 hour.

2 | Meanwhile, in a large bowl stir together garbanzo beans, mango, and onion. For dressing, in a small bowl whisk together lime juice, oil, cinnamon, salt, cumin, and cayenne pepper.

3 | Drain any water off bulgur. Add bulgur, dressing, and the 3 tablespoons mint to the bean mixture, stirring to mix well. Divide salad greens evenly among five serving plates. Top each with 1 cup of the bulgur mixture. Sprinkle with feta cheese. If desired, garnish with additional fresh mint.

Glass Noodle Salad with Peanut Sauce

Look for glass noodles, also called bean threads or cellophane noodles, in the Asian section of your supermarket.

SERVINGS 4 (1³/₄ cups each)
CARB. PER SERVING 41 g
PREP 20 minutes
STAND 15 minutes

1 3.75-ounce package bean threads (cellophane noodles)

2 cups frozen sweet soybeans (edamame), thawed

2 cups broccoli florets, cut up or sliced

³/₄ cup chopped red sweet pepper

¹/₄ cup finely chopped shallot

2 tablespoons peanut butter

1 tablespoon reduced-sodium soy sauce

1 tablespoon rice vinegar

2 teaspoons honey

1¹/₂ teaspoons grated fresh ginger

¹/₈ to ¹/₄ teaspoon crushed red pepper

¹/₄ cup lightly salted peanuts, chopped

Lime wedges (optional)

PER SERVING: 303 cal., 12 g total fat (1 g sat. fat), 0 mg chol., 208 mg sodium, 41 g carb. (6 g fiber, 8 g sugars), 12 g pro. Exchanges: 1 vegetable, 2 starch, 1 lean meat, 2 fat.

1 In a large glass bowl combine bean threads and thawed edamame; pour enough boiling water over to cover completely. Cover and let stand for 15 to 20 minutes or until edamame is tender. Drain well; rinse with cold water and drain again. Snip noodles five or six times. Return noodles and edamame to the bowl. Add broccoli, sweet pepper, and shallot to the noodle mixture; toss together.

2 For dressing, place peanut butter in a small microwave-safe bowl. Microwave on 100 percent power (high) about 40 seconds or until melted. Whisk in soy sauce, vinegar, honey, ginger, and crushed red pepper. Pour dressing over noodle mixture; toss to combine.

3 Divide among four serving plates or bowls. Sprinkle with peanuts. If desired, squeeze lime wedges over all.

Tricolor Bean and Rice Salad

This salad has something for everyone. It is chewy from the rice, crunchy from the veggies, and slightly spicy and tangy.

SERVINGS 6 (1¼ cups each)
CARB. PER SERVING 41 g
PREP 30 minutes

- 1 15-ounce can no-salt-added black beans, rinsed and drained
- 1 15-ounce can no-salt-added red kidney beans, rinsed and drained
- 1 15-ounce can no-salt-added Great Northern beans, rinsed and drained
- 1 cup cooked brown rice*
- 1 cup chopped yellow sweet pepper
- 1 cup chopped red sweet pepper
- 1 cup thinly bias-sliced carrots
- ¼ cup snipped fresh Italian (flat-leaf) parsley
- ½ cup white wine vinegar
- 3 tablespoons olive oil
- 2 cloves garlic, minced
- 1 teaspoon chili powder
- ¾ teaspoon salt
- ½ teaspoon black pepper
- ¼ cup chopped pimiento-stuffed green olives (optional)

1 In a large bowl combine beans, rice, sweet peppers, carrots, and parsley. In a screw-top jar combine vinegar, olive oil, garlic, chili powder, salt, and black pepper. Cover and shake well to combine. Pour dressing over bean mixture; toss to combine.

2 Serve immediately or cover and chill for up to 24 hours before serving. If desired, top each serving with some of the chopped green olives.

*TEST KITCHEN TIP: Use leftover brown rice, frozen cooked brown rice, or a pouch of cooked brown rice prepared according to package directions.

PER SERVING: 286 cal., 8 g total fat (1 g sat. fat), 0 mg chol., 356 mg sodium, 41 g carb. (14 g fiber, 4 g sugars), 12 g pro. Exchanges: 1 vegetable, 2 starch, 1 fat.

comforting
soups

Whether it's piping hot or chilling cold, each spoonful of soup

comforts and soothes. From chunky concoctions to creamy

mixtures, these soups are brimming with good-for-you

ingredients that dish up fresh-picked, just-made flavors.

Hearty Ham and Potato Soup

There is no need to peel the potatoes. The potato skin adds color and boosts nutrition.

SERVINGS 4 (1½ cups each)
CARB. PER SERVING 30 g
PREP 35 minutes
COOK 15 minutes

2 cups small cauliflower florets (about ½ inch in diameter)

2 tablespoons water

4 ounces extra-lean lower-sodium ham, chopped (¾ cup)

2 teaspoons canola oil

1 cup chopped red sweet pepper

2 cloves garlic, minced

8 ounces red potatoes, cut into ½-inch cubes

1¾ cups no-salt-added chicken broth

⅛ to ¼ teaspoon crushed red pepper

1 12-ounce can evaporated fat-free milk

1 tablespoon cornstarch

½ cup sliced green onions

2 tablespoons light butter or diet margarine

1 tablespoon snipped fresh sage

½ cup shredded reduced-fat sharp cheddar cheese (2 ounces)

1 In a small microwave-safe bowl combine cauliflower and the water. Cover with vented plastic wrap. Microwave on 100 percent power (high) for 3 to 5 minutes or until cauliflower is very tender. Cool slightly; drain. Place cooked cauliflower in a food processor or blender. Cover and process or blend until pureed. Set aside.

2 Meanwhile, in a large saucepan cook ham in 1 teaspoon of the hot oil over medium-high heat for 3 to 5 minutes or until lightly browned. Using a slotted spoon, remove ham from saucepan; set aside.

3 In the same large saucepan cook sweet pepper and garlic in the remaining 1 teaspoon hot oil for 3 minutes. Stir in potatoes, broth, and crushed red pepper. Bring to boiling over high heat; reduce heat. Simmer, covered, about 10 minutes or just until potatoes are tender.

4 In a small bowl combine evaporated milk and cornstarch, stirring until smooth. Add to saucepan; cook and stir until thickened and bubbly. Stir in ¼ cup of the green onions, the light butter, sage, ham, and pureed cauliflower. Cook over medium-low heat about 5 minutes to heat through and allow flavors to blend. Ladle soup into bowls to serve. Top with cheese and the remaining ¼ cup green onions.

20 grams pro.

PER SERVING: 296 cal., 11 g total fat (5 g sat. fat), 33 mg chol., 623 mg sodium, 30 g carb. (3 g fiber, 16 g sugars), 20 g pro. Exchanges: 1 milk, 1 starch, 1.5 lean meat, 1 fat.

Italian Meatball and Tortellini Soup

Stirring in a little basil pesto just before serving adds a fresh and flavorful dimension.

SERVINGS 8 (1^{1}/$_{2}$ cups each)
CARB. PER SERVING 28 g
PREP 20 minutes
SLOW COOK 6 hours (low) or 3 hours (high)

1 24-ounce package frozen Italian-style cooked turkey meatballs*

8 ounces fresh cremini mushrooms, sliced

2 medium carrots, sliced

1 medium onion, coarsely chopped

6 cups water

4 cups coarsely chopped, trimmed fresh kale or Swiss chard

1 9-ounce package refrigerated regular or whole wheat three-cheese tortellini

^{1}/$_{4}$ cup purchased basil pesto

1 In a 5- to 6-quart slow cooker combine meatballs, mushrooms, carrots, and onion. Pour water over all.

2 Cover and cook on low-heat setting for 6 to 8 hours or on high-heat setting for 3 to 4 hours.

3 If using low-heat setting, turn to high-heat setting. Add kale and tortellini to slow cooker. Cover and cook for 30 minutes more. Stir in pesto just before serving. Ladle soup into bowls to serve.

*TEST KITCHEN TIP: Choose a brand of frozen Italian-style cooked turkey meatballs that has 380 mg of sodium or less per 3-ounce serving (such as Foster Farms brand).

PER SERVING: 328 cal., 14 g total fat (4 g sat. fat), 55 mg chol., 623 mg sodium, 28 g carb. (3 g fiber, 5 g sugars), 24 g pro. Exchanges: 1 vegetable, 1.5 starch, 3 lean meat, 1 fat.

Mushroom and Beef Soup

Sirloin steak is a lean beef choice that doesn't require hours of simmering to become tender.

SERVINGS 6 (1^1/$_2$ cups each)
CARB. PER SERVING 11 g
PREP 30 minutes
COOK 25 minutes

- 12 ounces beef sirloin steak, trimmed
- 1 tablespoon canola oil
- 4 cups sliced assorted mushrooms, such as white, cremini, shiitake, and morel
- ^{1}/$_4$ cup chopped shallot
- 2 cloves garlic, minced
- 4 cups low-sodium beef broth
- 1 14.5-ounce can no-salt-added diced tomatoes, undrained
- 1 cup chopped carrot
- ^{1}/$_2$ cup chopped celery
- 1 bay leaf
- ^{1}/$_2$ teaspoon dried leaf thyme, crushed
- ^{1}/$_2$ teaspoon salt
- ^{1}/$_4$ teaspoon black pepper
- 2 cups loosely packed chopped fresh kale

PER SERVING: 139 cal., 5 g total fat (1 g sat. fat), 30 mg chol., 541 mg sodium, 11 g carb. (3 g fiber, 6 g sugars), 15 g pro. Exchanges: 2 vegetable, 1.5 lean meat, 0.5 fat.

1 Cut beef into ^{3}/$_4$-inch cubes. In a 4- to 5-quart Dutch oven heat oil over medium-high heat. Add beef and brown the meat. Remove beef; set aside. Add mushrooms, shallot, and garlic to pan. Cook for 4 to 5 minutes or until mushrooms are tender and lightly browned, stirring occasionally. Return beef to pan. Add broth, tomatoes, carrot, celery, bay leaf, thyme, salt, and pepper, stirring to loosen any browned bits from bottom of pan. Bring to boiling; reduce heat. Simmer, covered, for 20 to 25 minutes or until carrot is tender.

2 Stir in kale. Simmer for 5 to 10 minutes or until kale is tender. Discard bay leaf. Ladle soup into bowls to serve.

Turkey Posole

Poblano chiles and hominy add an unexpected and delicious twist to traditional chili.

SERVINGS 4 (2 cups each)
CARB. PER SERVING 30 g
PREP 15 minutes
COOK 28 minutes

2   teaspoons canola oil

1   pound ground turkey breast

¾   cup chopped red or green sweet pepper

½   cup chopped onion

½   cup chopped fresh poblano chile pepper*

2   teaspoons unsweetened cocoa powder

1   teaspoon dried oregano, crushed

½   teaspoon salt

½   teaspoon ground cumin

½   teaspoon ground ancho chile pepper

¼   teaspoon ground cinnamon

2   14.5-ounce cans no-salt-added diced tomatoes, undrained

1   15.5-ounce can golden hominy, rinsed and drained

1   cup water or reduced-sodium chicken broth

1   8-ounce can no-salt-added tomato sauce

¼   cup sliced green onions

¼   cup thinly sliced radishes

Lime wedges

1 In a 4-quart Dutch oven heat oil over medium heat. Add turkey, sweet pepper, onion, and poblano chile; cook until meat is no longer pink and vegetables are tender. Drain off fat. Stir in cocoa powder, oregano, salt, cumin, ancho chile pepper, and cinnamon. Cook and stir for 1 minute. Stir in tomatoes, hominy, water, and tomato sauce.

2 Bring to boiling; reduce heat. Simmer, covered, for 20 minutes to blend flavors, stirring occasionally. Ladle soup into bowls to serve. Garnish with green onions and radishes and serve with lime wedges.

*TEST KITCHEN TIP: Because chile peppers contain volatile oils that can burn your skin and eyes, avoid contact with them as much as possible. When working with chile peppers, wear plastic or rubber gloves. If your bare hands do touch the peppers, wash your hands and nails well with soap and warm water.

4 grams fat

PER SERVING: 271 cal., 4 g total fat (1 g sat. fat), 55 mg chol., 590 mg sodium, 30 g carb. (9 g fiber, 12 g sugars), 31 g pro. Exchanges: 1 vegetable, 1.5 starch, 3 lean meat.

QUICK TIP
No leftover chicken? To cook a skinless, boneless chicken breast, microwave it on a covered plate on 100 percent power (high) for 4 to 8 minutes or until no longer pink, turning the plate once.

Fresh Herb Chicken and Barley Soup

Shiitake mushrooms add a unique earthy flavor, but you can use any fresh mushrooms you like in their place.

SERVINGS 6 (1⅓ cups each)
CARB. PER SERVING 24 g
PREP 20 minutes
COOK 25 minutes

- 2 teaspoons olive oil
- 2 cups sliced fresh shiitake mushrooms
- 6 cups reduced-sodium chicken broth
- ¾ cup chopped red sweet pepper
- ½ cup quick-cooking barley
- 2 cups shredded or chopped cooked chicken or turkey
- 2 cups chopped asparagus
- 3 tablespoons snipped fresh chives
- 2 tablespoons snipped fresh marjoram or oregano or 2 teaspoons dried leaf marjoram or oregano, crushed
- ½ teaspoon black pepper

1 In a 4- to 5-quart Dutch oven heat oil over medium-high heat. Add mushrooms; cook for 4 minutes or until mushrooms are tender. Stir in broth, sweet pepper, and barley. Bring to boiling; reduce heat. Simmer, covered, about 15 minutes or until barley is tender. Stir in chicken, asparagus, chives, marjoram, and black pepper. Heat through. Ladle soup into bowls to serve.

PER SERVING: 220 cal., 5 g total fat (1 g sat. fat), 42 mg chol., 600 mg sodium, 24 g carb. (5 g fiber, 2 g sugars), 20 g pro. Exchanges: 1 vegetable, 1 starch, 2 lean meat, 0.5 fat.

Black-Eyed Pea Jambalaya

Chicken thighs have a robust taste that can stand up to the assertive flavors of andouille sausage and Cajun seasoning.

SERVINGS 6 (1$^{1}/_{3}$ cups jambalaya and $^{1}/_{3}$ cup cooked rice each)
CARB. PER SERVING 32 g
START TO FINISH 1 hour

8 ounces fresh or frozen small shrimp

8 ounces dried black-eyed peas

4 cups cold water

8 ounces skinless, boneless chicken thighs

4 ounces andouille or New Orleans-style sausage

2 teaspoons olive oil

$^{1}/_{2}$ cup chopped onion

$^{1}/_{2}$ cup chopped celery

$^{1}/_{2}$ cup chopped green sweet pepper

$^{1}/_{4}$ cup no-salt-added tomato paste

1 14.5-ounce can no-salt-added stewed tomatoes, undrained

1 cup reduced-sodium chicken broth

1 tablespoon salt-free Cajun or Creole seasoning

2 cups hot cooked brown rice

Green onions, thinly sliced

Snipped fresh parsley (optional)

Bottled hot pepper sauce (optional)

1 Thaw shrimp, if frozen. Peel and devein shrimp, leaving tails intact if desired. Rinse shrimp; pat dry with paper towels. Set aside. Rinse black-eyed peas. In a 4- to 5-quart Dutch oven combine black-eyed peas and the cold water. Bring to boiling; reduce heat. Simmer, covered, about 45 minutes or until black-eyed peas are tender; drain.

2 Meanwhile, cut chicken into $^{1}/_{2}$-inch pieces and cut sausage into $^{1}/_{4}$-inch slices; set aside. In a large skillet heat oil over medium heat. Add onion, celery, and sweet pepper. Cook for 5 to 7 minutes or until vegetables are tender, stirring occasionally. Add chicken and sausage to skillet. Cook and stir for 5 to 6 minutes or until starting to brown. Stir in tomato paste. Cook for 2 minutes more. Stir in tomatoes, broth, Cajun seasoning, and cooked black-eyed peas. Bring just to boiling. Stir in shrimp. Simmer for 2 to 3 minutes or until shrimp are opaque.

3 Ladle jambalaya over hot cooked rice in shallow bowls to serve. Garnish with green onions. If desired, sprinkle with parsley and pass hot pepper sauce.

PER SERVING: 274 cal., 7 g total fat (2 g sat. fat), 95 mg chol., 513 mg sodium, 32 g carb. (6 g fiber, 7 g sugars), 20 g pro. Exchanges: 2 starch, 2.5 lean meat.

20 grams pro.

Cold Cream of Cucumber Soup with Shrimp

Buttermilk and Greek yogurt make this hot-weather soup creamy and tangy.
It's a refreshing choice for a light dinner.

SERVINGS 4 (1½ cups each)
CARB. PER SERVING 17 g
START TO FINISH 25 minutes

2½ cups peeled, seeded, and chopped
cucumbers (about 2 medium)

2 cups buttermilk

1 cup plain fat-free Greek yogurt

⅓ cup chopped shallot

¼ cup fresh cilantro leaves

2 cloves garlic, minced

¼ teaspoon crushed red pepper

¼ teaspoon lemon-pepper seasoning

8 ounces frozen cooked, peeled
shrimp, thawed and coarsely
chopped

¼ cup thinly sliced radishes

2 tablespoons white balsamic
vinegar

½ cup coarsely chopped walnuts,
toasted

1 In a food processor combine 1½ cups of the cucumber,
the buttermilk, yogurt, shallot, cilantro, garlic, crushed
red pepper, and lemon-pepper seasoning. Cover and process
until mixture is smooth.

2 Transfer to a large bowl. Stir in the cold cooked shrimp,
radishes, balsamic vinegar, and the remaining 1 cup
chopped cucumber. Ladle soup into bowls to serve. Sprinkle
individual servings with walnuts.

17 grams carb.

PER SERVING: 270 cal., 12 g total fat (2 g sat. fat), 100 mg chol.,
346 mg sodium, 17 g carb. (2 g fiber, 13 g sugars), 25 g pro.
Exchanges: 0.5 milk, 1 vegetable, 3 lean meat, 1.5 fat.

Easy Butternut Squash Soup

If you have an immersion blender, use it to turn this soup into a golden puree right in the pan.

SERVINGS 4 (1 cup each)
CARB. PER SERVING 26 g
START TO FINISH 20 minutes

1 12-ounce package refrigerated cubed butternut squash

2 tablespoons water

½ cup finely chopped onion

2 tablespoons unsalted butter

1 14.5-ounce can reduced-sodium chicken broth

1 12-ounce can evaporated fat-free milk

1 teaspoon packed brown sugar

½ teaspoon kosher salt

½ teaspoon ground nutmeg

¼ to ½ teaspoon ground white pepper

Fresh thyme sprigs (optional)

Freshly grated nutmeg (optional)

1 Pour butternut squash package into a 2-quart microwave-safe baking dish with a lid. Add the 2 tablespoons water. Cover. Microwave on 100 percent power (high) for 3 minutes. Stir. Microwave for 3 minutes more. Stir again. Microwave about 2 minutes more or until squash is very tender. Using a pastry blender or potato masher, mash squash.

2 Meanwhile, in a heavy medium saucepan cook onion in hot butter until tender, stirring frequently.

3 In a food processor or blender combine cooked onions, mashed squash, broth, evaporated milk, brown sugar, salt, the ½ teaspoon ground nutmeg, and the white pepper. Cover and process or blend until smooth. Return soup to the saucepan. Cook and stir over medium-high heat until heated through. Ladle soup into bowls to serve. If desired, garnish with thyme and freshly grated nutmeg.

PER SERVING: 189 cal., 6 g total fat (4 g sat. fat), 15 mg chol., 606 mg sodium, 26 g carb. (3 g fiber, 16 g sugars), 9 g pro. Exchanges: 1 milk, 1 starch, 1 fat.

QUICK TIP
Look for packaged cubed butternut squash in the produce section of the supermarket.

Creamy Edamame-Veggie Soup

Surprise! No one will know that nutrient-rich tofu is blended into this soup to make it creamy and delicious.

SERVINGS 8 (³/4 cup soup each)
CARB. PER SERVING 8 g
START TO FINISH 30 minutes

1 tablespoon canola oil

½ cup chopped onion

4 cloves garlic, minced

2 cups reduced-sodium chicken broth

1½ cups small broccoli florets

1 cup frozen shelled sweet soybeans (edamame)

1 9-ounce package fresh spinach leaves

1 12.3-ounce package firm light silken-style tofu

1 6-ounce container plain fat-free Greek yogurt

½ teaspoon salt

½ teaspoon black pepper

¼ cup unsalted roasted soy nuts

2 tablespoons snipped fresh chives

1 In a 4-quart Dutch oven heat oil over medium heat. Add onion and garlic. Cook about 5 minutes or until onion is tender, stirring occasionally. Remove onion and garlic from the Dutch oven; set aside.

2 Add broth to the same Dutch oven. Bring to boiling. Add the broccoli and edamame. Return to boiling; reduce heat. Simmer, uncovered, for 3 to 5 minutes or just until broccoli is tender. Using a slotted spoon, transfer broccoli and edamame to a large bowl; set aside.

3 Add spinach to the hot broth mixture in Dutch oven. Cook and stir about 1 minute or until spinach begins to wilt. Remove from heat. Cool slightly. Stir broccoli mixture and onion mixture into spinach. Add spinach mixture and tofu, half at a time, to a blender or food processor. Cover and blend or process until very smooth.

4 Return all of the blended mixture to the Dutch oven. Add yogurt, salt, and pepper. Cook over medium-low heat just until heated through, stirring occasionally. Ladle soup into bowls to serve. Top with soy nuts and chives.

4 grams fat

PER SERVING: 106 cal., 4 g total fat (0 g sat. fat), 0 mg chol., 362 mg sodium, 8 g carb. (3 g fiber, 3 g sugars), 11 g pro. Exchanges: 0.5 starch, 1.5 lean meat.

sensational
sandwiches

Trade ho-hum filling-layered bread slices for a health-smart

lunchtime alternative. Let thins, tortillas, lettuce leaves, and

open-face sandwiches take center stage! Hot or cold and

stacked or rolled, this new collection is sure to give your family

a new favorite or two.

Asian Beef Cabbage Wraps

Jicama is super crunchy and has a slightly sweet flavor. Use a vegetable peeler to remove the skin.

SERVINGS 12 (1 wrap each)
CARB. PER SERVING 6 g
PREP 20 minutes
SLOW COOK 8 hours (low) or 4 hours (high) + 15 minutes (high)

1	2¾- to 3-pound boneless beef chuck pot roast
1½	cups chopped, peeled jicama or chopped celery
½	cup chopped green onions
¼	cup rice vinegar
¼	cup reduced-sodium soy sauce
2	tablespoons hoisin sauce
1	tablespoon grated fresh ginger
½	teaspoon salt
½	teaspoon chile oil
¼	teaspoon black pepper
2	tablespoons cornstarch
2	tablespoons cold water
12	savoy cabbage leaves
¼	cup coarsely chopped cashews (optional)
	Jicama strips (optional)
	Slivered green onions (optional)
	Crushed red pepper

PER SERVING: 214 cal., 12 g total fat (5 g sat. fat), 65 mg chol., 413 mg sodium, 6 g carb. (2 g fiber, 2 g sugars), 20 g pro. Exchanges: 1 vegetable, 3 lean meat, 1 fat.

1 Trim fat from meat. If necessary, cut meat to fit into a 3½- or 4-quart slow cooker. Place meat in the cooker. In a medium bowl combine chopped jicama, green onions, vinegar, soy sauce, hoisin sauce, ginger, salt, chile oil, and black pepper. Pour over meat.

2 Cover and cook on low-heat setting for 8 to 10 hours or on high-heat setting for 4 to 5 hours.

3 If using low-heat setting, turn cooker to high-heat setting. In a small bowl combine cornstarch and the cold water; stir into mixture in cooker. Cover and cook about 15 minutes more or until thickened.

4 Remove meat from cooker, reserving cooking juices. Using two forks, pull meat apart into shreds.

5 To assemble wraps, spoon shredded meat onto cabbage leaves. If desired, add cashews, additional jicama strips, and/or slivered green onions. Sprinkle with crushed red pepper. Fold in opposite sides of each cabbage leaf; roll up and secure with a pick. Serve wraps with the reserved cooking liquid for dipping.

Pesto Roast Beef Panini

If you haven't picked up cooked roast beef at your deli counter, you can shred leftover cooked roast beef to pile on.

SERVINGS 4 (1 sandwich each)
CARB. PER SERVING 25 g
START TO FINISH 15 minutes

- 3 tablespoons purchased basil pesto*
- 4 whole wheat sandwich rounds, split
- 4 slices ultrathin sliced provolone cheese
- 2 cups fresh spinch leaves
- 8 ounces low-fat, reduced-sodium sliced cooked roast beef
- 1 medium red or yellow sweet pepper, cut into thin strips

Nonstick cooking spray

1 To assemble sandwiches, spread pesto evenly on cut sides of sandwich rounds. On the bottom halves of sandwich rounds layer cheese, spinach, roast beef, and sweet pepper strips. Add tops of sandwich rounds.

2 Lightly coat a panini sandwich maker or unheated griddle with cooking spray. Preheat panini sandwich maker or preheat griddle over medium heat. Cook sandwiches for 3 to 5 minutes in the panini sandwich maker or 6 to 8 minutes on a griddle (if using a griddle, place a heavy skillet on sandwiches) or until cheese is melted and bread is golden brown, turning sandwiches once halfway through cooking if using a griddle.

*TEST KITCHEN TIP: To make your own pesto, in a food processor or blender place 2 cups packed fresh basil leaves; $1/2$ cup finely shredded Parmesan; $1/4$ cup olive oil; 3 tablespoons chopped toasted walnuts; 2 cloves garlic, minced; and $1/4$ teaspoon salt. Cover and process until smooth. Any extra pesto can be covered and refrigerated for up to 3 days or placed in an airtight container and frozen for up to 1 month.

QUICK TIP

If the packaged ultrathin cheese slices are not available in your supermarket, go to the deli counter and request provolone sliced as thinly as possible.

PER SERVING: 300 cal., 12 g total fat (4 g sat. fat), 47 mg chol., 501 mg sodium, 25 g carb. (6 g fiber, 4 g sugars), 25 g pro. Exchanges: 0.5 vegetable, 1.5 starch, 3 lean meat, 1 fat.

Chicken and Mushroom Bagel Sandwiches

The flavorful tomato-goat cheese spread adds a richness to every bite of these hot sandwiches.

SERVINGS 4 (1 sandwich each)
CARB. PER SERVING 28 g
PREP 20 minutes
COOK 10 minutes

2½ ounces goat cheese (chèvre)

¼ cup dried tomatoes (not oil-packed), cut into thin strips

2 tablespoons snipped fresh Italian (flat-leaf) parsley

1 small clove garlic, minced

⅛ teaspoon dried Italian seasoning, crushed

⅛ teaspoon black pepper

2 teaspoons olive oil

1 pound skinless, boneless chicken breast halves, cut into bite-size pieces or thin strips

8 ounces sliced fresh cremini mushrooms

4 100% whole wheat bagel thins, split and toasted

2 cups fresh arugula leaves

1 | In a food processor combine goat cheese, dried tomatoes, parsley, garlic, Italian seasoning, and pepper. Cover and process until smooth. Set aside.

2 | In a large skillet heat olive oil over medium-high heat. Add chicken; cook and stir about 5 minutes or until chicken is no longer pink. Reduce heat to medium. Add mushrooms; cook and stir about 5 minutes or until mushrooms are tender.

3 | To assemble sandwiches, evenly spread goat cheese mixture on cut sides of toasted bagel thins. Evenly divide chicken mixture and arugula among bottom halves of bagel thins. Add top halves of bagel thins.

36 grams pro.

PER SERVING: 349 cal., 12 g total fat (5 g sat. fat), 87 mg chol., 428 mg sodium, 28 g carb. (6 g fiber, 6 g sugars), 36 g pro. Exchanges: 1 vegetable, 1.5 starch, 4 lean meat, 0.5 fat.

Curry Chicken Salad Lettuce Wraps

Save on carbs by wrapping this sweet and crunchy chicken salad in tender lettuce leaves such as Boston or Bibb lettuce.

>> SERVINGS 2 (3 wraps each)
CARB. PER SERVING 21 g
START TO FINISH 15 minutes

1 5.3-ounce carton plain fat-free Greek yogurt

½ teaspoon curry powder

Dash black pepper

6 ounces seedless red grapes, halved

4 ounces refrigerated grilled chicken breast, chopped

½ cup chopped celery

2 tablespoons slivered almonds, toasted

6 lettuce leaves

Honey (optional)

1 In a medium bowl stir together yogurt, curry powder, and pepper. Add grapes, chicken, celery, and almonds; stir to combine.

2 To assemble wraps, divide the chicken mixture among the lettuce leaves. To eat, wrap the lettuce around the chicken mixture. If desired, drizzle filling with honey before wrapping.

PER SERVING: 219 cal., 5 g total fat (1 g sat. fat), 37 mg chol., 508 mg sodium, 21 g carb. (2 g fiber, 17 g sugars), 24 g pro. Exchanges: 1 fruit, 0.5 starch, 3 lean meat.

Apple-Brat Burgers

Applesauce is stirred into the burger mixture to help keep the burgers moist and add a slight sweetness.

SERVINGS 2 (1 patty, $^1/_2$ cup slaw, and 1 bun each)
CARB. PER SERVING 32 g
PREP 20 minutes
CHILL 2 hours
GRILL 14 minutes

1 egg white, lightly beaten

2 tablespoons fine dry whole wheat bread crumbs

2 tablespoons unsweetened applesauce

1 tablespoon finely chopped onion

$^1/_4$ teaspoon ground sage

$^1/_4$ teaspoon black pepper

$^1/_8$ teaspoon ground nutmeg

4 ounces lean ground pork

4 ounces uncooked ground turkey breast

2 light whole wheat hamburger buns, split and toasted

1 recipe Creamy Apple Slaw

PER SERVING: 366 cal., 11 g total fat (4 g sat. fat), 64 mg chol., 358 mg sodium, 32 g carb. (8 g fiber, 12 g sugars), 34 g pro. Exchanges: 2 starch, 4 lean meat, 1 fat.

1 In a large bowl combine egg white, bread crumbs, applesauce, onion, sage, pepper, and nutmeg. Add pork and turkey; mix well. Shape mixture into two $^3/_4$-inch-thick patties. Using your thumb, indent the middle of each patty.

2 For a gas or charcoal grill, place patties on the greased grill rack directly over medium heat. Cover and grill for 14 to 18 minutes or until done (165°F),* turning once halfway through grilling time.

3 To assemble burgers, place patties on bottom halves of buns. Top each with $^1/_2$ cup of the Creamy Apple Slaw and a bun top.

CREAMY APPLE SLAW: In a small bowl combine $^1/_4$ cup plain fat-free Greek yogurt and 1 teaspoon cider vinegar. Stir in $^1/_2$ cup coarsely shredded, peeled Granny Smith apple; $^1/_4$ cup shredded carrot; $^1/_4$ cup shredded red cabbage; and 1 tablespoon raisins. Cover and chill for 2 hours before serving.

*TEST KITCHEN TIP: The internal color of a burger is not a reliable doneness indicator. A turkey patty cooked to 165°F is safe, regardless of color. To measure the doneness of a patty, insert an instant-read thermometer through the side of the patty to a depth of 2 to 3 inches.

Turkey and Bean Wraps

Make sure the label says ground turkey breast. Plain ground turkey can contain dark meat and skin.

SERVINGS 8 (1 wrap each)
CARB. PER SERVING 27 g
PREP 25 minutes
BAKE 10 minutes

8 7- to 8-inch flour tortillas

1 pound ground turkey breast

1 cup chopped onion

2 cloves garlic, minced

1 cup no-salt-added black beans or pinto beans, rinsed and drained

½ cup bottled salsa

2 teaspoons chili powder

½ cup shredded cheddar cheese (2 ounces)

½ cup shredded lettuce

¼ cup sliced pitted ripe olives (optional)

Fresh pico de gallo (optional)

PER SERVING: 250 cal., 6 g total fat (3 g sat. fat), 35 mg chol., 412 mg sodium, 27 g carb. (15 g fiber, 1 g sugars), 22 g pro. Exchanges: 1.5 starch, 2.5 lean meat, 0.5 fat.

1 Preheat oven to 350°F. Stack tortillas; wrap in foil. Heat in the oven for 10 minutes to soften.

2 Meanwhile, for filling, in a large skillet cook turkey breast, onion, and garlic over medium heat until meat is browned and onion is tender, using a wooden spoon to break up meat. Drain off fat. Stir beans, salsa, and chili powder into meat mixture in skillet. Heat through.

3 To assemble wraps, spoon about ⅓ cup of the filling onto each tortilla; top each with 1 tablespoon cheese, 1 tablespoon lettuce, and a few olive slices (if using). Roll up tortillas. If desired, serve with pico de gallo.

Shrimp Tacos with Avocado Topper

Rather than creamy guacamole, this spicy avocado mixture is coarsley mashed for a more pleasing texture and look.

SERVINGS 2 (2 tacos each)
CARB. PER SERVING 31 g
START TO FINISH 25 minutes

- ½ of an avocado, seeded, peeled, and chopped
- 2 tablespoons fresh cilantro leaves
- 2 teaspoons finely chopped jalapeño chile pepper*
- ¼ teaspoon finely shredded lime peel
- 2 teaspoons lime juice
- ½ teaspoon chili powder
- 8 ounces fresh or frozen medium shrimp in shells
- 1 teaspoon olive oil
- 1 clove garlic, minced
- ½ teaspoon minced fresh ginger
- ⅛ teaspoon black pepper
- 4 6-inch white corn tortillas, warmed according to package directions
- ¾ cup packaged shredded cabbage with carrot (coleslaw mix)
- ⅓ cup chopped red sweet pepper
- 2 lime wedges

PER SERVING: 285 cal., 10 g total fat (1 g sat. fat), 143 mg chol., 589 mg sodium, 31 g carb. (7 g fiber, 3 g sugars), 20 g pro. Exchanges: 1 vegetable, 1.5 starch, 2 lean meat, 1 fat.

1 In a small bowl combine avocado, cilantro, chile pepper, lime peel, lime juice, and chili powder. Mash lightly with a fork; cover and set aside.

2 Thaw shrimp, if frozen. Peel, devein, and halve shrimp lengthwise. Rinse shrimp; pat dry with paper towels. In a small skillet heat olive oil over medium heat. Add garlic and ginger; cook and stir for 30 seconds. Add shrimp; sprinkle with the black pepper. Cook for 3 to 4 minutes or until shrimp are opaque.

3 To assemble tacos, place two tortillas on each of two serving plates. Divide coleslaw mix and sweet pepper among tortillas, leaving one side of each tortilla uncovered. Add warm shrimp; top with avocado mixture. Fold over each tortilla to form a taco. Serve with lime wedges.

*TEST KITCHEN TIP: Because chile peppers contain volatile oils that can burn your skin and eyes, avoid direct contact with them as much as possible. When working with chile peppers, wear plastic or rubber gloves. If your bare hands do touch the peppers, wash your hands and nails well with soap and warm water.

Fish Taco Wraps

If you prefer, spoon the salsa mixture over the assembled wraps instead of combining it with the sour cream as a dressing for the coleslaw mix.

SERVINGS 4 (1 wrap each)
CARB. PER SERVING 21 g
START TO FINISH 20 minutes

1 pound fresh or frozen skinless halibut fillets, ½ to ¾ inch thick

Olive oil nonstick cooking spray

1 teaspoon ancho chili powder or regular chili powder

¼ cup light sour cream

¼ cup fruit salsa (any flavor)

2 cups packaged shredded cabbage with carrot (coleslaw mix)

4 6- to 7-inch whole grain flour tortillas

Lime wedges (optional)

PER SERVING: 294 cal., 7 g total fat (2 g sat. fat), 40 mg chol., 450 mg sodium, 21 g carb. (11 g fiber, 5 g sugars), 32 g pro. Exchanges: 1 starch, 0.5 carb., 4 lean meat, 0.5 fat.

1 | Thaw fish, if frozen. Preheat broiler. Rinse fish; pat dry with paper towels. Measure thickness of fish fillets. Lightly coat the unheated rack of a broiler pan with cooking spray. Place fish on rack. Sprinkle with chili powder. Broil 4 to 5 inches from heat for 4 to 6 minutes per ½-inch thickness of fish or until fish flakes easily when tested with a fork. Cool fish slightly. Using a fork, flake fish into bite-size chunks.

2 | Meanwhile, in a medium bowl stir together sour cream and the ¼ cup salsa. Add the 2 cups cabbage mix; toss to coat.

3 | To assemble wraps, divide cabbage mixture among tortillas. Top with fish. Roll up tortillas. If desired, serve with lime wedges.

Tuna-Artichoke Open-Face Sandwiches

Top each sandwich with a few slivers of red onion for an extra crunch and a punch of flavor.

SERVINGS 4 (1 sandwich each)
CARB. PER SERVING 20 g
START TO FINISH 15 minutes

- 2 5-ounce cans low-sodium chunk light tuna in water, drained and flaked
- 8 pieces quartered marinated artichoke hearts, drained and coarsely chopped
- 2 tablespoons finely chopped red onion
- 2 tablespoons snipped fresh Italian (flat-leaf) parsley
- 2 tablespoons light mayonnaise
- 2 teaspoons olive oil
- 1½ teaspoons finely shredded lemon peel
- ½ teaspoon dried oregano, crushed
- ¼ teaspoon crushed red pepper
- Dash black pepper
- 4 slices pumpernickel bread, toasted
- 4 romaine lettuce leaves, torn into large pieces
- 1 medium tomato, thinly sliced

1 | In a medium bowl stir together tuna, artichoke hearts, onion, parsley, mayonnaise, olive oil, lemon peel, oregano, crushed red pepper, and black pepper.

2 | To assemble sandwiches, top toasted bread slices with romaine, tomato slices, and tuna mixture, dividing evenly.

PER SERVING: 202 cal., 7 g total fat (1 g sat. fat), 28 mg chol., 595 mg sodium, 20 g carb. (3 g fiber, 2 g sugars), 15 g pro. Exchanges: 1 vegetable, 1 starch, 1.5 lean meat, 1 fat.

Deviled Egg Vegetable Sandwiches

When combined with hummus and fresh chives, hard-cooked egg yolks create a sandwich spread similar to the filling of deviled eggs.

SERVINGS 4 (1 sandwich each)
CARB. PER SERVING 29 g
PREP 25 minutes

4 eggs

½ cup purchased hummus (such as plain, roasted pine nut, roasted red pepper, roasted garlic, or spicy)

1 tablespoon snipped fresh chives

1 6-ounce jar marinated artichoke hearts, drained and chopped

4 whole wheat sandwich thins, split and lightly toasted

2 leaves romaine lettuce, trimmed and halved

4 medium radishes, trimmed and thinly sliced

¼ medium cucumber, thinly sliced

1 To hard-cook eggs, place eggs in a single layer in a large saucepan (do not stack eggs). Add enough cold water to cover the eggs by 1 inch. Bring to a rapid boil over high heat (water will have large rapidly breaking bubbles). Remove from heat, cover, and let stand for 15 minutes; drain. Run cold water over the eggs or place them in ice water until just cool enough to handle; drain.

2 Peel eggs by gently tapping them on the countertop. Roll the egg between the palms of your hands. Peel off eggshell, starting at the large end. Cut eggs in half. Transfer three of the yolks to a small bowl. Discard the fourth yolk. Slice the egg whites.

3 Add hummus and chives to egg yolks in bowl. Mash and mix with a fork until well combined. Stir in chopped artichoke hearts.

4 To assemble sandwiches, spread hummus mixture on cut sides of toasted sandwich thins. Evenly divide lettuce, sliced egg whites, radishes, and cucumber slices among bottom halves of sandwich thins. Add top halves of sandwich thins.

PER SERVING: 262 cal., 12 g total fat (3 g sat. fat), 138 mg chol., 497 mg sodium, 29 g carb. (7 g fiber, 9 g sugars), 13 g pro.
Exchanges: 0.5 vegetable, 1.5 starch, 1.5 lean meat, 1.5 fat.

29 grams carb.

simple
sides and salads

Most consider the main dish to be the star of the meal. But

when fruits and vegetables are in peak season, they deserve the

attention. Pair these hot and cold nutrient-loaded dishes with

simple grilled, broiled, seared, or roasted meats, poultry, or fish

for stunning menus.

Asparagus-Snap Pea Stir-Fry

Preserve the flavor and color of garden-fresh vegetables in this quick-cooking sweet and crunchy stir-fry.

SERVINGS 6 (1 cup each)
CARB. PER SERVING 11 g or 10 g
START TO FINISH 25 minutes

1 pound fresh asparagus spears

1 tablespoon vegetable oil

2 teaspoons grated fresh ginger

2 cloves garlic, minced

1 medium red onion, cut into thin wedges

1 medium red sweet pepper, cut into 1-inch pieces

2 cups fresh or frozen sugar snap pea pods

1 tablespoon sesame seeds

2 tablespoons reduced-sodium soy sauce

2 tablespoons rice vinegar

1 tablespoon packed brown sugar*

1 teaspoon toasted sesame oil

1 Snap off and discard woody bases from asparagus. If desired, scrape off scales. Bias-slice asparagus into 2-inch pieces (you should have about 3 cups).

2 In a wok or large skillet heat vegetable oil over medium-high heat. Add ginger and garlic; cook and stir for 15 seconds. Add asparagus, onion, and sweet pepper; cook and stir for 3 minutes. Add pea pods and sesame seeds; cook and stir for 3 to 4 minutes more or until vegetables are crisp-tender.

3 Add soy sauce, rice vinegar, brown sugar, and sesame oil to vegetable mixture; toss to coat. If desired, serve with a slotted spoon.

*SUGAR SUBSTITUTE: Choose Splenda Brown Sugar Blend. Follow package directions to use product amount equivalent to 1 tablespoon packed brown sugar.

PER SERVING: 90 cal., 4 g total fat (0.5 g sat. fat), 0 mg chol., 189 mg sodium, 11 g carb. (3 g fiber, 7 g sugars), 3 g pro. Exchanges: 0.5 carb., 1.5 vegetable, 0.5 fat.

PER SERVING WITH SUBSTITUTE: Same as above, except 86 cal., 10 g carb. (6 g sugars), 188 mg sodium. Exchanges: 0 carb.

Green Beans and Petite Reds

If you can't finy tiny new potatoes, cut any red-skin potatoes into 1-inch pieces.

SERVINGS 8 (²/₃ cup each)
CARB. PER SERVING 17 g
PREP 20 minutes
SLOW COOK 4 hours (low) or 2 hours (high)

Nonstick cooking spray

1 pound fresh green beans, trimmed

1 pound tiny new potatoes, quartered

1 cup chopped onion

¼ cup water

¼ teaspoon salt

¼ teaspoon black pepper

¼ cup light mayonnaise

¼ cup fat-free sour cream

1 to 2 tablespoons fat-free milk

1 tablespoon Dijon-style mustard

1 tablespoon lemon juice

½ teaspoon dried tarragon, crushed

¼ teaspoon salt

Black pepper

1 | Coat a 3½- or 4-quart slow cooker with cooking spray. In the prepared cooker combine green beans, potatoes, onion, the water, ¼ teaspoon salt, and ¼ teaspoon pepper.

2 | Cover and cook on low-heat setting for 4 hours or on high-heat setting for 2 hours.

3 | Meanwhile, for sauce, in a small bowl whisk together mayonnaise, sour cream, milk, mustard, lemon juice, tarragon, and ¼ teaspoon salt. Cover with plastic wrap and chill until needed.

4 | To serve, stir the sauce into mixture in slow cooker, tossing until vegetables are coated. Sprinkle with additional pepper.

PER SERVING: 100 cal., 3 g total fat (1 g sat. fat), 3 mg chol., 265 mg sodium, 17 g carb. (3 g fiber, 4 g sugars), 3 g pro. Exchanges: 1 vegetable, 0.5 starch, 1 fat.

QUICK TIP
If you prefer a thinner sauce, stir in a little more fat-free milk, 1 tablespoon at a time.

Mediterranean Broccoli Medley

White balsamic vinegar does not discolor these vegetables as traditional red balsamic vinegar might, and it delivers all of the complex flavor.

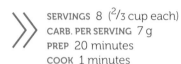

SERVINGS 8 (²/3 cup each)
CARB. PER SERVING 7 g
PREP 20 minutes
COOK 1 minutes

4 cups fresh broccoli florets

3¹/2 cups sliced fresh cremini or button mushrooms (8 ounces)

1 cup thinly bias-sliced carrots (2 medium)

1 cup coarsely chopped yellow summer squash (1 small)

1 tablespoon white balsamic vinegar or white wine vinegar

1 tablespoon olive oil

¹/2 teaspoon black pepper

¹/2 teaspoon Dijon-style mustard

¹/4 teaspoon salt

¹/3 cup snipped fresh basil

¹/2 cup crumbled reduced-fat feta cheese (2 ounces)

1 | Bring a large Dutch oven of water to boiling. Add broccoli, mushrooms, carrots, and summer squash to boiling water. Return to boiling. Cook for 1 to 2 minutes or just until crisp-tender; drain. Return vegetables to the pot.

2 | For vinaigrette, in a small bowl whisk together vinegar, olive oil, pepper, mustard, and salt. Add vinaigrette and basil to the cooked vegetables; toss to combine. Transfer vegetables to a serving bowl; sprinkle with feta cheese.

PER SERVING: 64 cal., 3 g total fat (1 g sat. fat), 2 mg chol., 205 mg sodium, 7 g carb. (2 g fiber, 3 g sugars), 4 g pro. Exchanges: 1.5 vegetable, 0.5 fat.

Corn and Edamame

Thanks to frozen vegetables, this colorful side dish can be made year-round.

SERVINGS 8 (^{3}/4 cup each)
CARB. PER SERVING 19 g
START TO FINISH 20 minutes

- 2 tablespoons olive oil
- 1 16-ounce package frozen whole kernel corn, thawed
- 1 cup chopped red sweet pepper
- 1 16-ounce package frozen sweet soybeans (edamame), thawed
- ^{1}/3 cup pitted ripe olives, sliced
- ^{1}/2 teaspoon salt
- ^{1}/2 teaspoon ground cumin
- ^{1}/2 teaspoon chili powder
- ^{1}/2 teaspoon black pepper
- ^{1}/4 cup snipped fresh cilantro
- 2 tablespoons lime juice
- 1 fresh jalapeño chile pepper, halved, seeded, and finely chopped (optional)*

PER SERVING: 163 cal., 7 g total fat (1 g sat. fat), 0 mg chol., 196 mg sodium, 19 g carb. (5 g fiber, 4 g sugars), 8 g pro. Exchanges: 1 starch, 0.5 lean meat, 1 fat.

1 In a large skillet heat olive oil over medium-high heat. Add corn and sweet pepper; cook and stir for 3 to 5 minutes or until sweet pepper is crisp-tender. Reduce heat to medium-low. Stir in edamame, olives, salt, cumin, chili powder, and black pepper. Cook for 2 to 3 minutes or until heated through, stirring occasionally. Remove from heat. Stir in cilantro and lime juice. If desired, top with fresh jalapeño.

*TEST KITCHEN TIP: Because chile peppers contain volatile oils that can burn your skin and eyes, avoid direct contact with them as much as possible. When working with chile peppers, wear plastic or rubber gloves. If your bare hands do touch the chile peppers, wash your hands and nails well with soap and warm water.

QUICK TIP
For a creamy alternative, substitute rinsed and drained canned lima beans or cannellini beans for the edamame.

Scalloped Root Veggies

Use the vegetables shown here or mix and match any combination of celery root, potatoes, parsnips, and turnips.

SERVINGS 6 ($^1/_2$ cup each)
CARB. PER SERVING 20 g
PREP 25 minutes
BAKE 55 minutes
STAND 10 minutes

Butter-flavor nonstick cooking spray

3 cups peeled, halved, and thinly sliced celery root (about 1 pound)

2 cups thinly sliced, peeled parsnips (about 12 ounces)

$^3/_4$ cup fat-free evaporated milk

2 tablespoons light butter with canola oil

1 teaspoon snipped fresh thyme leaves

1 clove garlic, minced

$^1/_4$ teaspoon black pepper

5 tablespoons finely shredded Parmesan cheese

2 teaspoons flour

Fresh thyme (optional)

PER SERVING: 129 cal., 3 g total fat (1 g sat. fat), 5 mg chol., 223 mg sodium, 20 g carb. (4 g fiber, 7 g sugars), 5 g pro. Exchanges: 1 starch, 1 fat.

1 Preheat oven to 375°F. Coat a 1$^1/_2$-quart oval baking dish or casserole with cooking spray. Arrange sliced celery root and parsnips in the prepared dish.

2 In a small saucepan combine milk, butter, the snipped thyme, the garlic, and pepper; heat over low heat just until simmering. Pour over vegetables in baking dish.

3 Bake, covered, for 40 minutes. Meanwhile, in a small bowl stir together 2 tablespoons of the Parmesan cheese and the flour. Stir flour mixture into vegetables. Sprinkle with the remaining 3 tablespoons Parmesan cheese. Bake, uncovered, about 15 minutes more or until vegetables are tender and top is lightly browned. Let stand for 10 minutes before serving. If desired, garnish with additional fresh thyme.

Spiced Sweet Potato Wedges

Make this popular restaurant side dish at home. Leave the skins on for extra fiber. Roasting makes the skins crisp and easy to bite.

SERVINGS 4 (4 wedges each)
CARB. PER SERVING 22 g or 21 g
PREP 10 minutes
ROAST 25 minutes

2 sweet potatoes (about 10 ounces each)

1 tablespoon olive oil

1 teaspoon packed brown sugar*

1/4 teaspoon kosher salt

1/4 teaspoon smoked paprika

1/4 teaspoon black pepper

1/4 teaspoon pumpkin pie spice

1/4 teaspoon hot chili powder

1 Preheat oven to 425°F. Place a baking sheet in the oven to preheat.

2 Scrub sweet potatoes; cut each potato lengthwise into 8 wedges (16 wedges total). In a large bowl drizzle potato wedges with olive oil; toss to coat. In a small bowl combine brown sugar, kosher salt, smoked paprika, pepper, pumpkin pie spice, and chili powder. Sprinkle spice mixture over sweet potato wedges; toss to coat.

3 Arrange wedges in a single layer on the hot baking sheet. Roast for 25 to 30 minutes or until potatoes are tender and browned, turning wedges once halfway through roasting time.

*SUGAR SUBSTITUTES: Choose from Splenda Brown Sugar Blend or Sugar Twin Granulated Brown. Follow package directions to use product amount equivalent to 1 teaspoon brown sugar.

PER SERVING: 124 cal., 3 g total fat (0 g sat. fat), 0 mg chol., 182 mg sodium, 22 g carb. (3 g fiber, 5 g sugars), 2 g pro. Exchanges: 1.5 starch, 0.5 fat.

PER SERVING WITH SUBSTITUTE: Same as above, except 123 cal., 21 g carb.

3 grams fat

Spinach-Basil Brown Rice Risotto

Let the slow cooker do some of the work when you are serving a crowd.

SERVINGS 10 (½ cup each)
CARB. PER SERVING 23 g
PREP 20 minutes
SLOW COOK 4 hours (low) or 2 hours (high)

Nonstick cooking spray

1½ cups uncooked brown rice

1 cup chopped red or green sweet pepper

¾ teaspoon salt

3½ cups water

2 cups packed fresh spinach, coarsely chopped (2 ounces)

¼ to ½ cup snipped fresh basil

¼ cup pine nuts or slivered almonds, toasted*

2 tablespoons olive oil

1 teaspoon grated lemon peel

1 clove garlic, minced

Fresh basil (optional)

Finely shredded lemon peel (optional)

PER SERVING: 158 cal., 6 g total fat (1 g sat. fat), 0 mg chol., 188 mg sodium, 23 g carb. (2 g fiber, 1 g sugars), 3 g pro. Exchanges: 1.5 starch, 1 fat.

1 Coat a 4-quart slow cooker with cooking spray. In the prepared cooker combine rice, sweet pepper, and salt. Pour the water over mixture in cooker.

2 Cover and cook on low-heat setting for 4 to 5 hours or on high-heat setting for 2 to 2½ hours or until rice is tender.

3 Add spinach, the snipped basil, the pine nuts, oil, the grated lemon peel, and the garlic to mixture in slow cooker, stirring until spinach is wilted. If desired, garnish with additional basil and finely shredded lemon peel.

*TEST KITCHEN TIP: To toast nuts, preheat oven to 350°F. Spread nuts in a shallow baking pan. Bake for 5 to 10 minutes or until light brown, watching carefully and stirring once or twice.

Vegetable Israeli Couscous

Can't find Israeli couscous? Use any tiny pasta in its place, such as orzo, acini de pepe, or ditalini.

SERVINGS 8 ($^1/_2$ cup each)
CARB. PER SERVING 17 g
PREP 25 minutes
COOK 20 minutes
CHILL 4 hours

- 1   cup Israeli couscous
- 1   medium yellow sweet pepper, coarsely chopped
- 1   medium zucchini, coarsely chopped
- 1   medium tomato, seeded and coarsely chopped
- 2   green onions, sliced
- 2   tablespoons lemon juice
- 2   tablespoons reduced-sodium chicken broth
- 1   tablespoon olive oil
- 1   tablespoon snipped fresh mint
- 1   clove garlic, minced
- $^1/_4$ teaspoon salt
- $^1/_4$ teaspoon black pepper
- $^1/_4$ cup crumbled feta cheese
-    Fresh mint leaves

PER SERVING: 109 cal., 3 g total fat (1 g sat. fat), 4 mg chol., 211 mg sodium, 17 g carb. (2 g fiber, 2 g sugars), 3 g pro. Exchanges: 0.5 vegetable, 1 starch.

1 In a large saucepan bring 2 quarts lightly salted water to boiling.

2 Meanwhile, in a medium skillet toast the couscous over medium heat about 7 minutes or until golden brown, stirring frequently.

3 Add the couscous to the boiling water. Cook for 7 minutes. Add sweet pepper and zucchini. Return to boiling and cook about 5 minutes more or until couscous is tender. Drain and transfer to a large bowl. Stir in the the tomato and green onions.

4 Meanwhile, in a small bowl mix together lemon juice, broth, olive oil, snipped mint, garlic, salt, and black pepper. Stir mixture into couscous mixture. Serve warm or cover and chill for up to 4 hours. To serve, sprinkle with feta cheese and garnish with fresh mint leaves.

Mixed Greens with Edamame, Almonds, and Dried Tomatoes

A few thin shavings of a high-quality cheese such as Parmigiano-Reggiano to finish a dish adds so much flavor.

SERVINGS 6 (²/₃ cup salad each)
CARB. PER SERVING 7 g
START TO FINISH 25 minutes

6 cups torn baby salad greens

½ cup dried tomatoes (oil-packed), drained and cut into pieces

½ cup fresh or frozen sweet soybeans (edamame), thawed if frozen

¼ cup blanched almonds, toasted and coarsely chopped

3 tablespoons lemon juice

2 tablespoons olive oil

¼ teaspoon freshly ground black pepper

Shaved Parmigiano-Reggiano cheese (optional)

1 In a large salad bowl combine salad greens, dried tomatoes, edamame, and almonds.

2 For dressing, in a small glass measuring cup whisk together lemon juice, oil, and pepper. To serve, pour dressing over salad and toss to coat. Divide salad among six individual salad plates. If desired, top each serving with a few shavings of Parmigiano-Reggiano cheese.

4 grams pro.

PER SERVING: 120 cal., 10 g total fat (1 g sat. fat), 0 mg chol., 33 mg sodium, 7 g carb. (3 g fiber, 1 g sugars), 4 g pro. Exchanges: 1 vegetable, 0.5 lean meat, 1.5 fat.

QUICK TIP

To toast almonds before chopping them, place them in a single layer in a shallow baking pan and bake in a 350°F oven for 5 to 10 minutes, shaking the pan occasionally.

Blackberry Salad with Feta

When blackberries are in season and you want to impress, indulge in this knockout salad.

SERVINGS 12 ($^1\!/_2$ cup berries, 1 tablespoon onions, and about 1 tablespoon feta cheese each)

CARB. PER SERVING 11 g

PREP 25 minutes

STAND 1 hour

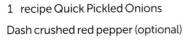

1 recipe Quick Pickled Onions

Dash crushed red pepper (optional)

6 to 8 cups fresh blackberries or blueberries

$^1\!/_3$ cup fresh mint leaves, large leaves torn

2 tablespoons turbinado sugar (raw sugar)*

2 teaspoons finely shredded lemon peel

3 tablespoons olive oil

4 ounces feta cheese, crumbled

PER SERVING: 99 cal., 6 g total fat (2 g sat. fat), 8 mg chol., 156 mg sodium, 11 g carb. (4 g fiber, 7 g sugars), 3 g pro. Exchanges: 0.5 fruit, 0.5 lean meat, 1 fat.

PER SERVING WITH SUBSTITUTE: Same as above, except 98 cal. and 6 g sugars.

1 Drain the Quick Pickled Onions. In a large bowl gently toss blackberries, mint, sugar, lemon peel, and the drained onions. Arrange on serving platter. Drizzle with the olive oil. Serve with feta cheese.

QUICK PICKLED ONIONS: Thinly sliver 1 small red onion. In a small bowl toss together onion, 3 tablespoons cider vinegar, 1 teaspoon granulated sugar,* $^1\!/_2$ teaspoon mustard seeds, and $^1\!/_4$ teaspoon salt. Cover; let stand at room temperature for 1 to 4 hours, stirring occasionally.

***SUGAR SUBSTITUTES:** We do not recommend using a sugar substitute for the turbinado sugar. For the granulated sugar in the pickled onions, choose from Splenda Granular, Equal Spoonful or packets, or Sweet'N Low bulk or packets. Follow package directions to use product amount equivalent to 1 teaspoon sugar.

Garden Three-Bean Salad with Fresh French Dressing

Three beans equals three textures: crisp-tender, chewy, and creamy.

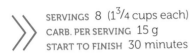

SERVINGS 8 (1³/₄ cups each)
CARB. PER SERVING 15 g
START TO FINISH 30 minutes

2 cups fresh green beans, trimmed if desired

¼ cup water

⅛ teaspoon salt

8 cups mixed salad greens

2 cups frozen sweet soybeans (edamame), thawed

1 cup canned no-salt-added cannellini beans (white kidney beans), rinsed and drained

1 cup radishes, sliced

1 recipe Fresh French Dressing

1 In a microwave-safe bowl combine green beans, the water, and salt. Toss to distribute salt among beans. Microwave, uncovered, on 100 percent power (high) for 3 to 5 minutes or until crisp-tender. Let stand at room temperature until cool; drain.

2 Place salad greens in a large salad bowl; add green beans, edamame, cannellini beans, and radishes. Add about half of the Fresh French Dressing; toss gently. Pass the remaining dressing.

FRESH FRENCH DRESSING: In a blender combine 2 medium tomatoes, halved and seeded; ¼ cup olive oil; 2 to 3 tablespoons red wine vinegar; 2 tablespoons tomato paste; 2 tablespoons snipped fresh tarragon; 2 teaspoons Dijon-style mustard; ⅛ teaspoon salt; and ⅛ teaspoon black pepper. Cover and blend until thoroughly mixed. Tomatoes vary in juiciness; if dressing is too thin, blend in additional tomato paste, 1 teaspoon at a time. Chill until serving time.

PER SERVING: 165 cal., 9 g total fat (1 g sat. fat), 0 mg chol., 169 mg sodium, 15 g carb. (6 g fiber, 4 g sugars), 7 g pro. Exchanges: 1 vegetable, 0.5 starch, 1.5 fat.

QUICK TIP

The Fresh French Dressing can be stored, covered, in an airtight container in the refrigerator for up to 3 days. Its name is also a delightful tongue-twister.

Potato-Kale Salad

Quickly blanching the kale in the potato water slightly tenderizes it and brightens the color.

SERVINGS 8 (³/4 cup each)
CARB. PER SERVING 15 g
PREP 20 minutes
COOK 12 minutes

- 1¼ pounds tiny red, golden, and/or purple new potatoes, halved or quartered
- 6 cups torn fresh kale
- ½ cup finely chopped onion
- ½ cup finely snipped fresh Italian (flat-leaf) parsley
- ¼ cup seasoned rice wine vinegar
- ¼ cup light sour cream
- 2 tablespoons light mayonnaise
- 2 tablespoons Dijon-style mustard
- ½ teaspoon black pepper
- ½ teaspoon celery seeds
- ¼ teaspoon celery salt or regular salt
- 1 hard-cooked egg, chopped

1 Place potatoes in a 4-quart Dutch oven. Add enough cold water to cover potatoes by 5 inches. Bring to boiling; reduce heat. Simmer, uncovered, about 12 minutes or until potatoes are fork-tender but not falling apart.

2 Add kale to potatoes in Dutch oven. Cook and stir for 30 seconds; drain. Return potatoes and kale to the Dutch oven. Cook, uncovered, over low heat for 3 to 4 minutes to evaporate excess moisture, stirring gently. Remove from heat; cool completely.

3 In a large bowl whisk together onion, parsley, vinegar, sour cream, mayonnaise, mustard, pepper, celery seeds, and celery salt. Fold chopped egg into sour cream mixture. Fold in potato-kale mixture. Serve immediately or cover and chill for up to 12 hours.

PER SERVING: 99 cal., 3 g total fat (1 g sat. fat), 27 mg chol., 210 mg sodium, 15 g carb. (2 g fiber, 2 g sugars), 3 g pro. Exchanges: 1 vegetable, 0.5 starch, 1 fat.

Farm Salad with Sweet Peppers and Sage Croutons

Did you know you can eat the flowers of fresh herbs, too? They add flavor and are a fun touch.

SERVINGS 12 (1$\frac{1}{2}$ cups each)
CARB. PER SERVING 17 g
PREP 30 minutes
ROAST 20 minutes
STAND 15 minutes

- 4 red sweet peppers
- 10 cups torn mixed salad greens
- 2 cups cherry tomatoes, halved
- $\frac{1}{2}$ cup small fresh sage leaves or torn large sage leaves
- 1 recipe Sage Croutons
- 1 recipe Cider Vinaigrette
- $\frac{1}{2}$ cup fresh herb flowers
- Fresh herb flowers (optional)

PER SERVING: 159 cal., 9 g total fat (1 g sat. fat), 0 mg chol., 285 mg sodium, 17 g carb. (2 g fiber, 4 g sugars), 4 g pro. Exchanges: 1 vegetable, 0.5 starch, 2 fat.

1 Preheat oven to 425°F. Cut peppers in half lengthwise; remove stems, seeds, and membranes. Place pepper halves, cut sides down, on a foil-lined baking sheet. Roast for 20 to 25 minutes or until peppers are charred and very tender. Bring foil up around peppers and fold edges together to enclose. Let stand about 15 minutes or until cool enough to handle. Using a sharp knife, gently pull off skin in strips and discard. Cut peppers into bite-size strips.

2 In a large salad bowl combine greens, tomatoes, sage, sweet pepper strips, and Sage Croutons. Drizzle with about half of the Cider Vinaigrette; toss to coat. Top with the $\frac{1}{2}$ cup herb flowers. Pass the remaining Cider Vinaigrette. If desired, garnish with additional herb flowers.

SAGE CROUTONS: Preheat oven to 425°F. Tear enough bread from a baguette to make 4 cups bite-size pieces (about 8 ounces bread). In a large bowl toss bread with 2 to 3 tablespoons olive oil, 2 tablespoons snipped fresh sage, $\frac{1}{2}$ teaspoon garlic powder, $\frac{1}{4}$ teaspoon salt, and $\frac{1}{4}$ teaspoon black pepper. Spread coated bread in a 15×10×1-inch baking pan. Bake about 10 minutes or until browned, stirring once.

CIDER VINAIGRETTE: In screw-top jar combine $\frac{2}{3}$ cup cider vinegar, $\frac{1}{3}$ cup olive oil, 1 tablespoon stone-ground mustard, 1 tablespoon honey, $\frac{1}{2}$ teaspoon salt, and $\frac{1}{4}$ teaspoon black pepper. Cover and shake well to combine.

eye-opening
breakfasts

Give each day a fresh start with nutritious breakfast dishes full

of fresh ingredients. From everyday favorites like frozen waffles

topped with fruit and toasted sandwiches to weekend specialties

like bicuits and gravy and egg casseroles, each is lightened up

just for you.

Frizzled Eggs over Garlic Steak and Mushroom Hash

If you have a long and active day ahead, this meaty breakfast is for you.
It will give you the energy you need to go the distance

SERVINGS 4 (½ cup hash, 1 egg, and
3 ounces steak each)
CARB. PER SERVING 22 g
START TO FINISH 30 minutes

2 tablespoons vegetable oil

2 cups frozen diced hash brown
potatoes with onions and peppers

1 8-ounce package sliced fresh
mushrooms

4 3-ounce thin breakfast steaks

¼ teaspoon salt

¼ teaspoon black pepper

4 cloves garlic, thinly sliced

4 eggs

Fresh tarragon (optional)

1 In a large skillet heat 1 tablespoon of the oil over medium-high heat. Add potatoes and mushrooms; cook, covered, for 10 minutes, stirring often. Remove potato mixture from skillet; cover to keep warm.

2 Sprinkle steaks with half of the salt and pepper. Heat the remaining 1 tablespoon oil in skillet. Add steaks and garlic; cook for 3 to 4 minutes for medium rare (145°F), turning once halfway through cooking time. Remove from skillet; cover to keep warm.

3 Break eggs into the hot skillet; sprinkle with the remaining salt and pepper. Reduce heat to low; cook eggs for 3 to 4 minutes or until whites are completely set and yolks start to thicken. Arrange potatoes, steaks, and eggs on four serving plates. If desired, garnish with fresh tarragon.

PER SERVING: 351 cal., 16 g total fat (3 g sat. fat), 233 mg chol., 295 mg sodium, 22 g carb. (2 g fiber, 1 g sugars), 30 g pro. Exchanges: 1 vegetable, 1 starch, 3.5 lean meat, 2 fat.

Vegetable-Filled Omelets

Substitute your favorite garden-fresh veggies for those suggested here. Make sure to use 1$\frac{1}{2}$ cups total to add to the tomatoes.

SERVINGS 4 (1 omelet with $\frac{1}{2}$ cup filling each)
CARB. PER SERVING 7 g
START TO FINISH 30 minutes

$\frac{1}{2}$ cup canned no-salt-added diced tomatoes with basil, garlic, and oregano, drained

$\frac{1}{2}$ cup chopped, seeded cucumber

$\frac{1}{2}$ cup chopped yellow summer squash

$\frac{1}{2}$ of a ripe avocado, seeded, peeled, and chopped

2 eggs

1 cup refrigerated or frozen egg product, thawed

2 tablespoons water

1 teaspoon dried basil, crushed

$\frac{1}{4}$ teaspoon salt

$\frac{1}{4}$ teaspoon black pepper

Nonstick cooking spray

$\frac{1}{4}$ cup shredded reduced-fat Monterey Jack cheese with jalapeño chile peppers (1 ounce)

Snipped fresh chives (optional)

PER SERVING: 128 cal., 6 g total fat (2 g sat. fat), 97 mg chol., 357 mg sodium, 7 g carb. (3 g fiber, 4 g sugars), 12 g pro. Exchanges: 1 vegetable, 1.5 lean meat, 1 fat.

1 For filling, in a medium bowl stir together tomatoes, cucumber, squash, and avocado. Set aside.

2 In a medium bowl whisk together eggs, egg product, the water, basil, salt, and pepper. For each omelet, coat an unheated small nonstick skillet generously with cooking spray. Heat skillet over medium heat. Add a generous $\frac{1}{3}$ cup of the egg mixture to hot skillet. Quickly begin stirring eggs gently but continuously with a wooden spatula until mixture resembles cooked egg pieces surrounded by liquid egg. Stop stirring. Cook for 30 to 60 seconds more or until egg is set. Spoon $\frac{1}{2}$ cup of the filling over one side of the omelet. Carefully fold omelet over the filling. Very carefully remove omelet from skillet. Repeat to make four omelets total, using paper towels to wipe skillet clean and spraying with cooking spray between omelets.

3 Sprinkle 1 tablespoon of the cheese over each omelet. If desired, garnish with chives.

Huevos Rancheros Tacos

Tacos aren't just for dinner. Use eggs and beans instead of beef for a protein-packed breakfast that won't weigh you down.

SERVINGS 4 (2 tacos each)
CARB. PER SERVING 31 g
START TO FINISH 25 minutes

2 teaspoons olive oil

½ cup chopped red onion

2 cloves garlic, minced

1 15-ounce can no-salt-added pinto beans, drained

½ teaspoon ground cumin

¼ teaspoon kosher salt

¼ teaspoon dried oregano, crushed

⅛ teaspoon cayenne pepper

½ cup water

Nonstick cooking spray

3 eggs

9 egg whites

8 6-inch corn tortillas, warmed*

½ cup shredded reduced-fat Colby and Monterey Jack cheese (2 ounces)

½ cup refrigerated pico de gallo

1 | In a large nonstick skillet heat oil over medium heat. Add onion; cook about 4 minutes or until softened. Add garlic; cook for 30 seconds more. Remove from heat. Stir beans, cumin, kosher salt, oregano, and cayenne pepper into the onion mixture, mashing the beans with the back of a spoon. Return to heat and stir in the water, continuing to mash the beans with the spoon. Simmer until beans are thick and spreading consistency (mixture won't be completely smooth). Remove bean mixture from skillet; keep warm.

2 | Rinse and dry the skillet. Coat the skillet with cooking spray. Heat skillet over medium heat. In a large bowl whisk together eggs and egg whites. Add egg mixture to skillet and cook, without stirring, until eggs begin to set on bottom and around edges. With a spatula or large spoon, lift and fold the partially cooked egg mixture so the uncooked portion flows underneath. Continue cooking for 2 to 3 minutes or until cooked through but still glossy and moist.

3 | To serve, spread bean mixture on warmed tortillas; top with cooked eggs. Sprinkle with cheese. Fold tacos in half. Top with pico de gallo.

*TEST KITCHEN TIP: To warm tortillas, place tortillas between paper towels. Microwave on 100 percent power (high) for 20 to 40 seconds. (Or preheat oven to 350°F. Wrap tortillas in foil. Bake for 10 minutes.)

22 grams pro.

PER SERVING: 325 cal., 12 g total fat (4 g sat. fat), 155 mg chol., 421 mg sodium, 31 g carb. (6 g fiber, 3 g sugars), 22 g pro. Exchanges: 2 starch, 2 lean meat, 1 fat.

QUICK TIP
Purchased shredded
reduced-fat cheese and a
refrigerated pico de gallo
save time and get you
out the door quicker.

Egg and Vegetable Muffins

This muffin or mini quiche is a delicious way to ensure you start the day without overeating.

SERVINGS 6 (2 muffins each)
CARB. PER SERVING 9 g
PREP 20 minutes
COOK 17 minutes
BAKE 15 minutes
COOL 5 minutes

Nonstick cooking spray

²/₃ cup water

¹/₃ cup bulgur

1 tablespoon olive oil

³/₄ cup chopped zucchini

¹/₄ cup chopped onion

¹/₂ cup crumbled reduced-fat feta cheese (2 ounces)

1 small tomato, cored, seeded, and chopped (¹/₃ cup)

2 cups refrigerated or frozen egg product, thawed, or 8 eggs, lightly beaten

2 teaspoons snipped fresh oregano and/or rosemary

¹/₈ teaspoon black pepper

PER SERVING: 117 cal., 4 g total fat (1 g sat. fat), 3 mg chol., 294 mg sodium, 9 g carb. (2 g fiber, 3 g sugars), 11 g pro. Exchanges: 0.5 vegetable, 0.5 starch, 1.5 lean meat, 0.5 fat.

1 Preheat oven to 350°F. Coat twelve 2¹/₂-inch muffin cups with cooking spray; set aside. In a small saucepan combine water and bulgur. Bring to boiling; reduce heat. Simmer, covered, for 12 to 15 minutes or until bulgur is tender. Drain off any liquid.

2 In a large skillet heat oil over medium heat. Add zucchini and onion. Cook for 5 to 10 minutes or until just tender, stirring occasionally. Remove from the heat and stir in bulgur, cheese, and tomato. Spoon mixture evenly into prepared muffin cups.

3 In a large bowl whisk together eggs, oregano, and pepper. Pour evenly over vegetable mixture in muffin cups.

4 Bake for 15 to 18 minutes or until a knife inserted in center of muffins comes out clean. Cool in muffin cups on a wire rack for 5 minutes. Run a thin knife around the edges of the muffins to loosen. Carefully remove muffins from the muffin cups. Serve warm.

Smoked Salmon Breakfast Wraps

Here's a flavorful way to start the day. You can nibble on a wrap as you walk out the door.

SERVINGS 4 (1 wrap each)
CARB. PER SERVING 14 g
START TO FINISH 20 minutes

⅓ cup light cream cheese spread

1 tablespoon snipped fresh chives

1 teaspoon finely shredded lemon peel

1 tablespoon lemon juice

4 6- to 7-inch whole wheat flour tortillas

3 ounces thinly sliced smoked salmon (lox-style), cut into strips

1 zucchini

Lemon wedges (optional)

1 In a small bowl stir together cream cheese spread, chives, lemon peel, and lemon juice until smooth. Spread evenly over tortillas, leaving a ½-inch border around the edges.

2 Divide salmon among tortillas, placing it on the bottom half of each tortilla. To make zucchini ribbons, draw a sharp vegetable peeler lengthwise along the zucchini to cut very thin slices. Place zucchini ribbons over salmon. Starting from the bottom, roll up tortillas. Cut each wrap in half. If desired, serve with lemon wedges.

14 grams carb.

PER SERVING: 124 cal., 6 g total fat (2 g sat. fat), 15 mg chol., 451 mg sodium, 14 g carb. (9 g fiber, 2 g sugars), 12 g pro. Exchanges: 1 starch, 1 lean meat.

Sweet Pepper and Hash Brown Baked Eggs

This easy breakfast casserole has a crowd-pleasing presentation and waistline-pleasing ingredients.

SERVINGS 8 (1 egg in pepper ring and ½ cup hash browns each)
CARB. PER SERVING 18 g
PREP 15 minutes
BAKE 35 minutes

Nonstick cooking spray

1 20-ounce package refrigerated shredded hash brown potatoes with peppers and spices

1 tablespoon olive oil

1 large green sweet pepper

½ cup pizza sauce

¼ cup finely shredded Parmesan cheese (1 ounce)

8 eggs

Freshly ground black pepper or snipped fresh basil (optional)

1 | Preheat oven to 375°F. Coat a 3-quart rectangular baking dish with cooking spray. Add potatoes to prepared baking dish. Drizzle oil over potatoes; toss to combine. Spread potatoes evenly in the baking dish. Bake for 10 minutes. Stir potatoes; spread evenly in the baking dish again. Bake for 10 minutes more.

2 | Meanwhile, slice the large green pepper into eight ¼- to ½-inch-thick rings. Remove seeds from slices. Remove potatoes from oven. Reduce oven temperature to 350°F. Arrange pepper rings in two rows on top of the potatoes. Spread 1 tablespoon of the pizza sauce within each pepper ring, then break an egg into each pepper ring. Top each egg with a rounded teaspoon of the shredded Parmesan cheese. Bake for 15 to 20 minutes more or until egg whites are set and yolks begin to thicken but are not hard.

3 | If desired, sprinkle with freshly ground black pepper and/or basil.

PER SERVING: 179 cal., 7 g total fat (2 g sat. fat), 188 mg chol., 491 mg sodium, 18 g carb. (2 g fiber, 2 g sugars), 9 g pro. Exchanges: 1 starch, 1 medium-fat meat, 0.5 fat.

7 grams fat

Biscuits and Country Sausage Gravy

Turkey breakfast sausage is a lean option in this classic biscuits and gravy combo.

SERVINGS 4 (½ cup gravy and 1 biscuit each)
CARB. PER SERVING 30 g
START TO FINISH 15 minutes

4 ounces uncooked bulk turkey breakfast sausage

1 tablespoon butter

2 tablespoons flour

¼ teaspoon black pepper

⅛ teaspoon salt

1½ cups fat-free milk

4 Cheddar Biscuits

Fresh sage leaves (optional)

1 In a medium saucepan cook sausage over medium heat until browned, using a wooden spoon to break up meat as it cooks. Add butter to saucepan. Stir until butter is melted. Stir in flour, pepper, and salt. Cook and stir for 1 minute. Whisk in milk. Cook and stir until thickened and bubbly. Cook and stir for 1 minute more.

2 Split each Cheddar Biscuit; place each split biscuit on a serving plate. Serve sausage mixture over split biscuits. If desired, garnish with fresh sage.

CHEDDAR BISCUITS: Preheat oven to 425°F. In a large bowl stir together 1¾ cups flour, 2 teaspoons baking powder, and ¼ teaspoon salt. Using a pastry blender, cut in 2 tablespoons cut-up cold butter, 2 tablespoons plain fat-free Greek yogurt, and 1 tablespoon canola oil. Stir in ¼ cup reduced-fat shredded cheddar cheese (1 ounce). Make a well in the center of the flour mixture. Add ⅔ cup fat-free milk all at once.

Turn dough out onto a lightly floured surface. Knead dough by folding and gently pressing it just until dough holds together. Pat dough into an 8½x4½-inch rectangle. Cut dough lengthwise in half. Cut each half crosswise into four biscuits. Place the eight biscuits 1 inch apart on an ungreased baking sheet.

Bake about 14 miutes or until golden brown. Serve warm. To store, place cooled biscuits in an airtight container. Cover and store in the refrigerator for up to 2 days or freeze for up to 2 months.

PER SERVING: 275 cal., 11 g total fat (5 g sat. fat), 41 mg chol., 558 mg sodium, 30 g carb. (1 g fiber, 6 g sugars), 14 g pro. Exchanges: 2 starch, 1 lean meat, 1.5 fat.

PER BISCUIT: 159 cal., 6 g total fat (3 g sat. fat), 11 mg chol., 253 mg sodium, 22 g carb. (1 g fiber, 1 g sugars), 5 g pro. Exchanges: 1.5 starch, 1 fat.

Cocoa Almond French Toast

Dark cocoa powder-covered almonds are a nutritious and delicious pairing.

SERVINGS 2 (2 slices bread, 1 tablespoon syrup, and 2 tablespooons raspberries each)
CARB. PER SERVING 29 g
START TO FINISH 10 minutes

½ cup unsweetened almond milk

⅓ cup refrigerated or frozen egg product, thawed

½ teaspoon ground cinnamon

½ teaspoon ground nutmeg

¼ cup dark chocolate-flavor almonds, finely chopped (1½ ounces)

Nonstick cooking spray

4 slices light whole wheat bread

2 tablespoons sugar-free chocolate-flavor syrup

¼ cup fresh raspberries

1 In a shallow dish beat together almond milk, egg, cinnamon, and nutmeg. Set aside ½ tablespoon of the almonds for garnish. Place remaining almonds in another shallow dish.

2 Coat a griddle* with cooking spray; heat griddle over medium heat. Meanwhile, dip each bread slice in the egg mixture for about 10 seconds per side. Dip soaked bread in the almonds, turning to coat both sides.

3 Cook almond-coated bread slices on hot griddle for 4 to 6 minutes or until golden brown, turning once halfway through cooking time. Cut slices in half diagonally. Arrange on two serving plates.

4 Drizzle chocolate syrup over the bread slices; top with raspberries. Sprinkle with the reserved almonds.

*TEST KITCHEN TIP: If you do not have a griddle, coat a large skillet with nonstick cooking spray; continue as directed, except cook half of the bread slices at a time.

PER SERVING: 250 cal., 12 g total fat (1 g sat. fat), 0 mg chol., 391 mg sodium, 29 g carb. (8 g fiber, 4 g sugars), 15 g pro. Exchanges: 0.5 fruit, 1.5 starch, 1.5 lean meat, 1 fat.

Strawberries and Cream Pancakes

A generous spoonful of juiced-up strawberries over these pancakes stands in for the typical sugar-laden syrup.

SERVINGS 12 (2 pancakes, 1 tablespoon cream cheese, and $^1/_4$ cup strawberries each)
CARB. PER SERVING 22 g
PREP 20 minutes
STAND 20 minutes
COOK 2 minutes per batch

3 cups coarsely chopped fresh strawberries

1 tablespoon finely shredded orange peel

$^1/_4$ cup orange juice

1 cup whole wheat pastry flour

$^1/_2$ cup all-purpose flour

$^1/_4$ cup oat flour or oat bran

2 tablespoons chia seeds or flaxseeds

1 tablespoon sugar*

1 tablespoon baking powder

$^1/_4$ teaspoon salt

1$^1/_2$ cups fat-free milk

$^1/_4$ cup refrigerated or frozen egg product, thawed, or 1 egg, lightly beaten

2 tablespoons canola oil

$^3/_4$ cup whipped Greek cream cheese,** softened

1 to 2 tablespoons orange juice

1 In a medium bowl combine strawberries, orange peel, and $^1/_4$ cup orange juice. Cover and let stand for 20 to 30 minutes to blend flavors, stirring occasionally.

2 In a large bowl stir together flours, seeds, sugar, baking powder, and salt. In another bowl use a fork to combine milk, egg, and oil. Add egg mixture all at once to flour mixture. Stir just until moistened (batter should be slightly lumpy).

3 For each pancake, pour 2 tablespoons batter onto a hot, lightly greased griddle or heavy skillet. Spread batter to an even layer if necessary. Cook over medium heat for 1 to 2 minutes on each side or until pancakes are golden brown; turn over when surfaces are bubbly and edges are slightly dry. Keep pancakes warm in a 200°F oven while making the rest.

4 To serve, in a small bowl combine cream cheese and 1 to 2 tablespoons orange juice; spread evenly over pancakes. Top with strawberries.

*TEST KITCHEN TIP: We do not recommend using a sugar substitute for this recipe.

**TEST KITCHEN TIP: If you cannot find the Greek cream cheese, make your own. In a small bowl stir together $^1/_2$ cup softened light tub-style cream cheese with $^1/_4$ cup plain fat-free Greek yogurt until smooth.

5 grams fat

PER SERVING: 158 cal., 5 g total fat (1 g sat. fat), 8 mg chol., 242 mg sodium, 22 g carb. (3 g fiber, 7 g sugars), 6 g pro. Exchanges: 1.5 starch, 1 fat.

Maple Berry-Topped Waffles

Sprinkle a combination of fresh berries on these waffles for a colorful antioxidant punch.

SERVINGS 2 (1 waffle, $1/4$ cup berries, 3 tablespoons yogurt, and 1 tablespoon syrup each)
CARB. PER SERVING 26 g
START TO FINISH 10 minutes

- 2 frozen 7-grain waffles, such as Kashi brand
- $1/2$ cup fresh blueberries, blackberries, and/or raspberries
- 6 tablespoons plain fat-free Greek yogurt
- 2 tablespoons light pancake syrup

PER SERVING: 143 cal., 3 g total fat (0 g sat. fat), 0 mg chol., 239 mg sodium, 26 g carb. (5 g fiber, 13 g sugars), 6 g pro. Exchanges: 0.5 milk, 1 starch, 0.5 carb.

1 | Toast waffles according to package directions.

2 | Meanwhile, in a small bowl combine half of the berries, the yogurt, and pancake syrup. Divide the yogurt mixture between the toasted waffles; sprinkle with the remaining berries.

QUICK TIP
Fresh berries aren't in season? Try sliced bananas or some dried fruit and toasted nuts instead.

Peanut Butter and Banana Breakfast Sandwich

Elvis fried his favorite sandwich, but you can skip that! This protein- and fiber-packed combo will satisfy you all morning.

>> **SERVINGS** 1 (1 sandwich)
CARB. PER SERVING 35 g
START TO FINISH 10 minutes

- **2** slices 100% whole wheat bread (about 45 calories per slice)
- **4** teaspoons reduced-fat natural-style creamy peanut butter
- **1** small banana or ½ of a medium banana, sliced

1 | Toast bread. While toast is still warm, spread 2 teaspoons of the peanut butter on each slice. Arrange banana slices on top of the peanut butter on one of the toast slices. Top with the other toast slice, peanut butter side down, to make a sandwich.

12 grams pro.

PER SERVING: 269 cal., 9 g total fat (1 g sat. fat), 0 mg chol., 237 mg sodium, 35 g carb. (8 g fiber, 11 g sugars), 12 g pro. Exchanges: 1 fruit, 1 starch, 1 medium-fat meat.

Apple Streusel Muffins

These muffins are like handheld coffee cakes. The recipe makes 12, so freeze a few for later in a freezer container for up to 3 months.

SERVINGS 12 (1 muffin each)
CARB. PER SERVING 26 g or 21 g
PREP 25 minutes
BAKE 18 minutes
COOL 5 minutes

Nonstick cooking spray

1 cup all-purpose flour

1 cup whole wheat flour or white whole wheat flour

1/3 cup packed brown sugar*

2 1/2 teaspoons baking powder

1 1/4 teaspoons apple pie spice

1/4 teaspoon salt

1 cup buttermilk

1/2 cup refrigerated or frozen egg product, thawed, or 2 eggs, lightly beaten

2 tablespoons canola oil

3/4 cup shredded, peeled apple (1 medium)

2 tablespoons finely chopped pecans

1 tablespoon flaxseed meal or toasted wheat germ

1 tablespoon packed brown sugar*

1 tablespoon butter

1 Preheat oven to 375°F. Lightly coat twelve 2 1/2-inch muffin cups with cooking spray; set aside. In a large bowl stir together all-purpose flour, whole wheat flour, the 1/3 cup brown sugar, the baking powder, apple pie spice, and salt. Make a well in the center of the flour mixture; set aside.

2 In a medium bowl combine buttermilk, egg, and oil. Add egg mixture all at once to flour mixture; stir just until moistened (batter should be lumpy). Fold in shredded apple. Spoon batter into prepared muffin cups, filling each about three-fourths full.

3 In a small bowl combine pecans, flaxseed meal, and the 1 tablespoon brown sugar. Using a pastry blender, cut in butter until mixture resembles coarse crumbs. Sprinkle pecan mixture on top of muffin batter in cups.

4 Bake for 18 to 20 minutes or until a toothpick inserted in centers comes out clean. Cool in muffin cups on a wire rack for 5 minutes. Remove muffins from muffin cups. Serve warm.

*SUGAR SUBSTITUTES: Choose from Sweet'N Low Brown or Sugar Twin Granulated Brown. Follow package directions to use product amount equivalent to 1/3 cup brown sugar in the muffins. We do not recommend using sugar substitute for the 1 tablespoon brown sugar in the topping.

PER SERVING: 220 cal., 5 g total fat (1 g sat. fat), 42 mg chol., 600 mg sodium, 24 g carb. (5 g fiber, 2 g sugars), 20 g pro. Exchanges: 1 vegetable, 1 starch, 2 lean meat, 0.5 fat.

PER SERVING WITH SUBSTITUTE: Same as above, except 142 cal., 21 g carb. (4 g sugars), 200 mg sodium. Exchanges: 0 carb.

good-for-you
snacks

Keeping your blood glucose levels in check between hearty

meals is easy when you snack right. Try one of these healthful

treats. Some are designed to make and eat now. Others can

be made and stashed so they are ready when you want

a quick bite.

Mango and Black Bean Salsa Cups

Enjoy a taste of the tropics with this salsa. If you can't find fresh mango and papaya, look for them refrigerated in jars in the produce section.

SERVINGS 16 ($^1\!/\!_4$ cup salsa and 8 scoop chips each)
CARB. PER SERVING 18 g
PREP 20 minutes

1 15-ounce can no-salt-added black beans, rinsed and drained

1 medium papaya, halved, seeded, peeled, and chopped (1$^1\!/\!_4$ cups)

1 medium mango, halved, peeled, pitted, and chopped (1 cup)

1 medium orange, sectioned and chopped

$^1\!/\!_3$ cup chopped red onion

2 tablespoons orange juice

2 tablespoons olive oil

2 tablespoons snipped fresh cilantro or parsley

1 tablespoon lime juice

$^1\!/\!_2$ teaspoon salt

$^1\!/\!_4$ teaspoon black pepper

$^1\!/\!_8$ to $^1\!/\!_4$ teaspoon cayenne pepper (optional)

8 ounces scoop-shape baked tortilla chips

Cilantro or parsley leaves (optional)

1 In a large bowl combine beans, papaya, mango, orange, and red onion. In a small bowl whisk together orange juice, olive oil, snipped cilantro, lime juice, salt, black pepper, and, if desired, cayenne pepper. Spoon orange juice mixture over bean mixture; toss to combine. Serve immediately or cover and chill for up to 24 hours.

2 To serve, spoon salsa into baked scoop chips. If desired, garnish cups with fresh cilantro or parsley leaves.

5 grams fat

PER SERVING: 126 cal., 5 g total fat (1 g sat. fat), 0 mg chol., 132 mg sodium, 18 g carb. (3 g fiber, 4 g sugars), 3 g pro. Exchanges: 0.5 fruit, 0.5 starch, 1 fat.

QUICK TIP
Section and chop the oranges over a dish to catch the juice. You should be able to reserve enough juice for the 2 tablespoons needed in the recipe.

Toasted Chickpeas

Enjoy a handful of crisp, flavorful toasted chickpeas instead of high-fat chips. You'll love how easy they are to make.

SERVINGS 6 (2½ tablespoons each)
CARB. PER SERVING 14 g
PREP 15 minutes
BAKE 32 minutes

1   15-ounce can no-salt-added garbanzo beans (chickpeas), drained

4   teaspoons olive oil

½   teaspoon paprika

¼   teaspoon salt

¼   teaspoon garlic powder

¼   teaspoon ground cumin

⅛   teaspoon black pepper

Dash cayenne pepper

1 Preheat oven to 450° F. Rub garbanzo beans with a paper towel to dry well and to remove the thin skins. Place in a 9x9x2-inch baking pan. Drizzle with olive oil; stir to coat.

2 Roast, uncovered, for 20 minutes, stirring once. Remove from oven and stir. Sprinkle with paprika, salt, garlic powder, cumin, black pepper, and cayenne pepper. Stir to coat evenly. Return to oven. Roast for 12 to 14 minutes more or until dried and crispy, stirring once. Cool completely before eating. Chickpeas can be stored in an airtight container overnight.

PER SERVING: 104 cal., 4 g total fat (0 g sat. fat), 0 mg chol., 115 mg sodium, 14 g carb. (3 g fiber, 0 g sugars), 4 g pro. Exchanges: 1 starch, 0.5 fat.

Chickpea Deviled Eggs

Eggs are rich in protein, so they make a satisfying snack—especially when you can have three egg halves per serving!

SERVINGS 12 (3 egg halves each)
CARB. PER SERVING 11 g or 9 g
START TO FINISH 30 minutes

18 hard-cooked eggs

1 15- to 16-ounce can garbanzo beans (chickpeas), rinsed and drained

¼ cup finely chopped celery

2 to 3 tablespoons plain fat-free Greek yogurt

2 tablespoons sugar*

2 tablespoons sliced green onion

2 tablespoons lemon juice

1 tablespoon yellow mustard

1 tablespoon water

1 teaspoon snipped fresh Italian (flat-leaf) parsley

½ teaspoon salt

¼ teaspoon celery seeds

Sliced green onion, sliced grape tomatoes, and/or quartered cucumber slices (optional)

Pita chips (optional)

1 | Halve hard-cooked eggs lengthwise and remove yolks. Set whites aside. Place three of the egg yolks in a food processor. Discard the other yolks.

2 | Add garbanzo beans, celery, yogurt, sugar, the 2 tablespoons green onion, the lemon juice, yellow mustard, the water, parsley, salt, and celery seeds to the yolks in food processor. Cover and process until smooth.

3 | Fill each egg white half with 2 teaspoons of the garbanzo bean mixture.

4 | If desired, garnish with additional green onion, grape tomatoes, and/or cucumber. If desired, serve with pita chips.

*SUGAR SUBSTITUTES: Choose from Splenda Granular, Truvia spoonable or packets, or Sweet'N Low bulk or packets. Follow package directions to use product amount equivalent to 2 tablespoons sugar.

PER SERVING: 100 cal., 2 g total fat (0 g sat. fat), 46 mg chol., 273 mg sodium, 11 g carb. (0 g fiber, 3 g sugars), 9 g pro. Exchanges: 0.5 starch, 0.5 carb., 1 lean meat.

PER SERVING WITH SUBSTITUTE: Same as above, except 93 cal., 9 g carb. (1 g sugars). Exchanges: 0 carb., 0.5 lean meat.

Pumpkin Spice Dip

This recipe serves a crowd. It would make a perfect contribution to an office food day.

SERVINGS 16 (2 tablespoons dip, 1/4 of an apple, and 3 pretzel twists each)
CARB. PER SERVING 18 g
PREP 10 minutes

3 ounces reduced-fat cream cheese (Neufchâtel), softened

3/4 cup canned pumpkin

1 6-ounce carton vanilla fat-free yogurt

2 tablespoons packed brown sugar*

1 teaspoon pumpkin pie spice

4 apples, sliced

48 honey-wheat braided pretzel twists

QUICK TIP
Freeze leftover canned pumpkin in a resealable plastic freezer bag. Thaw it in the refrigerator before using.

PER SERVING: 93 cal., 2 g total fat (1 g sat. fat), 4 mg chol., 116 mg sodium, 18 g carb. (2 g fiber, 8 g sugars), 2 g pro. Exchanges: 1 starch.

1 | In a medium bowl beat cream cheese with an electric mixer until light and fluffy. Beat in pumpkin, yogurt, brown sugar, and pumpkin pie spice. Serve dip with apple slices and pretzel twists.

*TEST KITCHEN TIP: We do not recommend using a sugar substitute for this recipe.

Spicy Crunch Mix

If you can't find the crunchy chickpeas for this mix, increase
the puffed corn cereal to 3 cups.

SERVINGS 14 (1/2 cup each)
CARB. PER SERVING 20 g
PREP 15 minutes
BAKE 30 minutes

- 2 cups puffed corn cereal
- 2 cups bite-size corn square cereal
- 2 cups whole grain or whole wheat melba toast rounds, coarsely broken (3 ounces)
- 3 tablespoons canola oil
- 3 tablespoons honey
- 3 tablespoons reduced-sodium Worcestershire sauce
- 1 teaspoon smoked paprika
- 1 teaspoon bottled hot pepper sauce
- 1 cup crunchy chipotle- or falafel-flavored chickpeas
- 1/2 cup shelled roasted, salted pistachio nuts

PER SERVING: 148 cal., 6 g total fat
(1 g sat. fat), 0 mg chol., 195 mg sodium,
20 g carb. (2 g fiber, 6 g sugars), 4 g pro.
Exchanges: 1 vegetable, 1 starch, 1 fat.

1 Preheat oven to 300°F. In a 13×9×2-inch baking pan combine cereals and melba toast rounds; set aside.

2 In a small bowl stir together the oil, honey, Worcestershire sauce, paprika, and hot pepper sauce. Pour oil mixture over cereal mixture in pan; toss until well coated.

3 Bake for 30 minutes, stirring twice. Stir in chickpeas and pistachio nuts. Spread snack mix on a large sheet of foil and let cool.

Brown Sugar-Cinnamon Cream Cheese Bagels

If you would rather not get out the electric mixer and if you don't mind a coarser texture, stir the cream cheese mixture with a fork until combined.

SERVINGS 8 (½ of a mini bagel, 1 tablespoon cream cheese mixture, and 1 tablespoon granola each)
CARB. PER SERVING 22 g
PREP 15 minutes
CHILL up to 2 hours

½ cup light tub-style cream cheese, softened

2 tablespoons fresh blueberries, mashed slightly

1½ tablespoons packed brown sugar*

¼ teaspoon ground cinnamon

4 whole wheat mini bagels, split and toasted

½ cup low-fat granola

1 In a small bowl combine cream cheese, slightly mashed blueberries, brown sugar, and cinnamon. Beat with an electric mixer on medium speed until well combined. Cover and chill for up to 2 hours. Stir before using.

2 Spread on toasted mini bagel halves. Top each bagel half with 1 tablespoon granola.

*TEST KITCHEN TIP: We do not recommend using a sugar substitute for this recipe.

PER SERVING: 133 cal., 3 g total fat (2 g sat. fat), 10 mg chol., 191 mg sodium, 22 g carb. (3 g fiber, 8 g sugars), 5 g pro. Exchanges: 1.5 starch, 0.5 fat.

5 grams pro.

QUICK TIP
Spread the cream cheese mixture on freshly toasted bagel halves. The cream cheese will melt slightly into the still-warm bagels.

Toasted PB&J Snacks

If you have a grill pan, you can use it to cook this family-friendly snack on the stove top.

SERVINGS 8 (1 kabob each)
CARB. PER SERVING 14 g
PREP 10 minutes
GRILL 3 minutes

- ¼ cup peanut butter
- 4 slices firm-texture whole wheat bread
- 2 tablespoons strawberry spreadable fruit
- 1 large banana

Nonstick cooking spray

PER SERVING: 106 cal., 5 g total fat (1 g sat. fat), 0 mg chol., 87 mg sodium, 14 g carb. (2 g fiber, 6 g sugars), 4 g pro. Exchanges: 1 starch, 1 fat.

1 Divide peanut butter between two of the bread slices, spreading evenly. Spread 1 tablespoon of the spreadable fruit on top of the peanut butter on each slice. Top with the two remaining bread slices, pressing firmly to make sandwiches. Cut each sandwich into eight squares. Cut banana into 16 slices.

2 Using eight 6- to 8-inch skewers,* alternately thread two sandwich squares and 2 banana slices on each skewer. Coat sandwich squares and banana with cooking spray.

3 For a charcoal or gas grill, place skewers on the grill rack directly over medium-low heat. Cover and grill for 3 to 4 minutes or until warm, turning every minute to brown evenly.

*TEST KITCHEN TIP: If using wooden skewers, soak in enough water to cover for 30 minutes; drain before using.

Blueberry Oat-Chia Seed Muffins

Tiny chia seeds are nutritional big dogs. They are high in fiber, antioxidants, and omega-3 fatty acids to name a few benefits.

SERVINGS 18 (2 mini muffins each)
CARB. PER SERVING 15 g or 13 g
PREP 20 minutes
BAKE 10 minutes

Nonstick cooking spray

1¼	cups flour
¾	cup regular rolled oats
⅓	cup sugar*
2	tablespoons chia seeds, ground
2	teaspoons baking powder
¼	teaspoon salt
1	egg, beaten
¾	cup fat-free milk
¼	cup vegetable oil
¾	cup fresh blueberries

PER SERVING: 108 cal., 4 g total fat (1 g sat. fat), 11 mg chol., 95 mg sodium, 15 g carb. (1 g fiber, 5 g sugars), 2 g pro. Exchanges: 1 starch, 0.5 fat.

PER SERVING WITH SUBSTITUTE: Same as above, except 102 cal., 13 g carb. (3 g sugars).

1 Preheat oven to 350°F. Lightly coat thirty-six 1¾-inch muffin cups with cooking spray or line with mini paper bake cups; set aside. In a large bowl combine flour, oats, sugar, chia seeds, baking powder, and salt. Make a well in the center of flour mixture; set aside.

2 In another bowl combine egg, milk, and oil. Add egg mixture all at once to flour mixture. Stir just until moistened (batter should be lumpy). Fold in blueberries.

3 Spoon a scant tablespoon batter into each prepared muffin cup, filling each two-thirds full. Bake about 10 minutes or until a toothpick inserted in centers comes out clean. Cool in muffin cups on a wire rack for 5 minutes. Remove muffins from muffin cups. Serve warm or at room temperature. Serve within one day of preparation.

*SUGAR SUBSTITUTES: Choose from Splenda Sugar Blend for Baking or Equal Sugar Lite. Follow package directions to use product amount equivalent to ⅓ cup sugar.

QUICK TIP
For easy cleanup, line muffin cups with paper bake cups. They also help keep muffins moist.

Crisp Apple Chips

Fruit chips are a popular snack. Making your own is easy and ensures you don't have added fat or sodium.

SERVINGS 4 (¼ apple [about ¾ ounce chips] each)
CARB. PER SERVING 31 g ro 19 g
PREP 20 minutes
BAKE 2 hours

2 large apples, such as Braeburn, Jazz, Pink Lady, or Gala, cored

¼ cup sugar*

2 teaspoons apple pie spice**

1 | Preheat oven to 200°F. Line two or three baking sheets with parchment paper; set aside.

2 | Using a mandoline or a serrated knife, cut apples crosswise into ⅛-inch slices. Arrange slices in a single layer on baking sheets. In a small bowl combine sugar and apple pie spice. Sprinkle apple slices with half of the sugar mixture. Use a pastry brush to brush mixture over apple slices to cover evenly. (Or place the sugar mixture in a small sieve; holding the sieve over the apple slices, stir the mixture with a spoon to evenly disperse the sugar mixture over the apples.) Turn apple slices and repeat with remaining sugar mixture.

3 | Bake for 2 to 2½ hours or until crisp, turning apple slices and rotating pans every 30 minutes. Cool completely on wire racks. Store apple slices in an airtight container for up to 1 week.

*SUGAR SUBSTITUTES: Choose from Splenda Sugar Blend for Baking or C&H Light Sugar and Stevia Blend. Follow package directions to use product amount equivalent to ¼ cup sugar.

**TEST KITCHEN TIP: If desired, substitute 1¼ teaspoons ground cinnamon, ¼ teaspoon ground cloves, ¼ teaspoon ground nutmeg, and ¼ teaspoon ground allspice for the apple pie spice.

PER SERVING: 116 cal., 0 g total fat, 0 mg chol., 2 mg sodium, 31 g carb. (3 g fiber, 25 g sugars), 0 g pro. Exchanges: 1 fruit, 1 carb.

PER SERVING WITH SUBSTITUTE: Same as above, except 67 cal., 19 g carb. (13 g sugars). Exchanges: 0 carb.

Berry Yogurt Parfaits

These parfaits are not only a satisfying snack, they are great for breakfast, too.

SERVINGS 4 ($^{1}/_{4}$ cup yogurt, $^{1}/_{3}$ cup berries, and $^{1}/_{4}$ cup cereal each)
CARB. PER SERVING 27 g
PREP 20 minutes

- 1 cup plain fat-free Greek yogurt
- 2 tablespoons honey
- 1 teaspoon vanilla
- $^{1}/_{2}$ teaspoon finely shredded lemon peel
- $^{1}/_{2}$ cup fresh raspberries
- $^{1}/_{2}$ cup fresh blackberries, halved if desired
- $^{1}/_{2}$ cup fresh blueberries
- 1 cup multigrain oats and honey cereal

  Lemon peel strips

PER SERVING: 129 cal., 0 g total fat, 0 mg chol., 75 mg sodium, 27 g carb. (4 g fiber, 18 g sugars), 6 g pro. Exchanges: 0.5 milk, 0.5 fruit, 1 starch.

1 | In a small bowl combine yogurt, honey, vanilla, and shredded lemon peel. (If desired, the yogurt mixture can be stirred together ahead of time, covered, and chilled for several hours.)

2 | Divide half of the yogurt mixture among four glasses or parfait dishes. Top with half of the berries and half of the cereal. Repeat layers. Serve immediately or cover and chill for up to 30 minutes. Garnish servings with lemon peel strips.

Frozen Fruit Cups

Pull out any partial containers of fruit you have in your refrigerator to make these frosty treats.

SERVINGS 8 ($^{1}/_{2}$ cup each)
CARB. PER SERVING 13 g or 10 g
PREP 15 minutes
FREEZE 4 hours
STAND 30 minutes

2   cups chopped cantaloupe

2   cups coarsley chopped fresh strawberries

1   cup fresh raspberries

1   cup fresh blackberries, halved

2   tablespoons sugar*

$^{1}/_{2}$ teaspoon finely shredded lemon peel

PER SERVING: 53 cal., 0 g total fat, 0 mg chol., 7 mg sodium, 13 g carb. (3 g fiber, 10 g sugars), 1 g pro. Exchanges: 1 fruit.

PER SERVING WITH SUBSTITUTE: Same as above, except 41 cal., 10 g carb. (6 g sugars).

QUICK TIP
Choose fruit that is in season. Use any combination of berries to equal 4 cups and/or substitute peaches or nectarines for cantaloupe.

1 In a large bowl combine cantaloupe, strawberries, raspberries, blackberries, sugar, and lemon peel. Transfer 2 cups of the mixture to a food processor. Cover and process until mixture is smooth. Return to whole fruit mixture and gently stir together.

2 Divide mixture into eight 4-ounce individual storage containers or small glasses or paper cups. Freeze for 4 to 24 hours or until frozen.

3 To serve, let frozen mixture stand for 30 to 40 minutes or until slightly thawed and slushy.**

*SUGAR SUBSTITUTES: Choose from Splenda Granular, Equal bulk or packets, or Sweet'N Low bulk or packets. Follow package directions to use product amount equivalent to 2 tablespoons sugar.

**TEST KITCHEN TIP: To serve frozen cups more quickly, dip the bottom of an individual container into hot water for 30 seconds. Transfer one serving to a small microwave-safe bowl. Microwave on 100 percent power (high) for 45 seconds to 1 minute or until partially thawed, breaking up with a fork after 30 seconds.

Tropical Smoothies

As bananas get ripe, slice, freeze, and store them in a resealable plastic bag so they're ready when you want a smoothie. This recipe uses about $^1/_2$ cup slices.

SERVINGS 4 ($^3/_4$ cup each)
CARB. PER SERVING 25 g
PREP 15 minutes
FREEZE 4 hours

1 small banana, peeled and cut up

3 cups frozen mixed fruit blend (pineapple, strawberries, mango, and/or peaches)

1 6-ounce carton vanilla or coconut fat-free yogurt

$^3/_4$ to 1 cup diet tropical blend carrot-based drink

Pineapple wedges (optional)

1 | Freeze banana pieces in a resealable freezer bag about 4 hours or until frozen.

2 | In a blender combine frozen banana and frozen fruit blend. Add yogurt and $^3/_4$ cup of the tropical drink. Cover and blend until smooth, adding more tropical drink as needed to reach desired consistency. Divide mixture among four glasses. If desired, garnish each serving with a pineapple wedge.

TEST KITCHEN TIP: For single-serving smoothies, prepare recipe and freeze in individual portions. Let individual portions stand at room temperature about 20 minutes before serving, stirring occasionally after mixture begins to thaw.

PER SERVING: 107 cal., 0 g total fat, 3 mg chol., 33 mg sodium, 25 g carb. (2 g fiber, 19 g sugars), 2 g pro. Exchanges: 1 fruit, 0.5 starch.

0 grams fat

delightful
desserts

You *can* finish a meal or celebrate the day with a little something

sweet. Choose one of these yummy treats that have been

trimmed in calories, carbohydrate, and fat to fit into your meal

plan. With an assortment this good, you're sure to find something

to satisfy your sweet tooth.

Cinnamon-Spiced Cake

Pureed cantaloupe gives this lovely cake a subtle melon flavor and also keeps it nice and moist.

SERVINGS 16 (1 slice cake and 1 tablespoon topping each)
CARB. PER SERVING 27 g or 26 g
PREP 30 minutes
BAKE 50 minutes
COOL 10 minutes

Nonstick cooking spray

1/2 cup chopped pecans (2 ounces)

1 tablespoon sugar*

1/2 teaspoon ground cinnamon

2 1/2 cups chopped cantaloupe (11 ounces)

1 package 2-layer-size sugar-free yellow cake mix

3/4 cup refrigerated or frozen egg product, thawed

1/3 cup water

2 tablespoons canola oil

1 teaspoon ground cinnamon

1 teaspoon vanilla extract or vanilla-butter-and-nut flavoring

1/2 teaspoon ground nutmeg

1/2 teaspoon ground ginger

1 cup frozen light whipped dessert topping, thawed

Ground cinnamon (optional)

1 Preheat oven to 325°F. Lightly coat a 10-inch fluted tube pan with cooking spay. Sprinkle pecans in the bottom of the prepared pan; set aside. In a small bowl stir together sugar and the 1/2 teaspoon cinnamon; set aside.

2 Place cantaloupe in a blender or food processor. Cover and blend or process until smooth. In a large bowl combine dry cake mix, cantaloupe puree, egg, the water, oil, the 1 teaspoon cinnamon, the vanilla, nutmeg, and ginger. Beat with an electric mixer on medium speed about 2 minutes or until well mixed.

3 Carefully pour batter over pecans in the tube pan; spread batter evenly. Bake for 50 to 55 minutes or until a toothpick inserted in center comes out clean.

4 Cool in pan on a wire rack for 10 minutes. Remove from pan. Immediately sprinkle with the sugar-cinnamon mixture. Cool completely before serving. Spoon whipped topping over slices. If desired, sprinkle with additional cinnamon.

*SUGAR SUBSTITUTES: Choose from Splenda Granular, Equal Spoonful or packets, Sweet'N Low bulk or packets, or Truvia. Follow package directions to use product amount equivalent to 1 tablespoon sugar.

PER SERVING: 158 cal., 7 g total fat (2 g sat. fat), 0 mg chol., 237 mg sodium, 27 g carb. (1 g fiber, 4 g sugars), 2 g pro. Exchanges: 1.5 starch, 1 fat.

PER SERVING WITH SUBSTITUTE: Same as above, except 156 cal., 26 g carb. (3 g sugars).

Lemon-Poppy Seed Angel Cake

Make sure your electric mixer beaters are absolutely clean so you get the most volume from the egg whites in this light and tangy cake.

SERVINGS 16 (1 slice each)
CARB. PER SERVING 28 g
PREP 20 minutes
BAKE 30 minutes

12 egg whites (1½ cups)
1 teaspoon cream of tartar
½ cup sugar*
2 tablespoons poppy seeds
1 teaspoon finely shredded lemon peel
2 teaspoons lemon juice
½ teaspoon vanilla
¼ teaspoon yellow food coloring
1 cup cake flour
½ cup sugar*
1 recipe Lemon Glaze
Frozen light whipped dessert topping, thawed (optional)
Finely shredded lemon peel (optional)

PER SERVING: 129 cal., 1 g total fat (0 g sat. fat), 0 mg chol., 42 mg sodium, 28 g carb. (0 g fiber, 20 g sugars), 4 g pro. Exchanges: 1 starch, 1 carb.

1 Preheat oven to 350°F. In a large bowl combine egg whites and cream of tartar. Beat with an electric mixer on medium-high speed for 1 to 2 minutes or until frothy. Reduce speed to medium; gradually add ½ cup sugar. Increase speed to medium-high; beat egg whites until soft peaks form (tips curl). Add poppy seeds, the 1 teaspoon lemon peel, the lemon juice, vanilla, and food coloring. Beat for 2 minutes more.

2 In a separate bowl sift together cake flour and ½ cup sugar. Using a rubber spatula, gently fold one-fourth of the flour mixture into the egg whites. Repeat three times, folding in the remaining flour mixture one-fourth at a time.

3 Pour cake batter into an ungreased 10-inch tube pan. Bake for 30 to 35 minutes or until cake top is lightly golden and springs back when lightly touched. Immediately invert cake in pan; cool completely. Loosen sides of cake from pan; remove cake from pan. Just before serving, pour Lemon Glaze over cake. If desired, serve with spoonfuls of dessert topping sprinkled with additional finely shredded lemon peel.

LEMON GLAZE: In a small bowl combine 1 cup powdered sugar,* 2 teaspoons finely shredded lemon peel, and 2 tablespoons lemon juice. Whisk until smooth. Pour over cake when ready to serve.

*****TEST KITCHEN TIP:** We do not recommend using sugar substitutes for this recipe.

Zucchini Cupcakes with Greek Yogurt Frosting

Quinoa is an unexpectedly delicious way to add a little nutritional bump to a tasty dessert.

SERVINGS 12 (1 cupcake each)
CARB. PER SERVING 24 g
PREP 20 minutes
COOL 1 hour
BAKE 20 minutes

Nonstick cooking spray

1 cup whole wheat flour

1/4 cup granulated sugar*

1/4 cup packed brown sugar*

1 teaspoon ground cinnamon

1/2 teaspoon baking powder

1/2 teaspoon salt

1/4 teaspoon baking soda

2 eggs

1/4 cup fat-free milk

1 cup cooked quinoa**

1 cup shredded zucchini

1/2 cup unsweetened applesauce

1/4 cup canola oil

1 teaspoon vanilla

1 recipe Greek Yogurt Frosting

1/2 to 1 teaspoon finely shredded lemon peel

1 Preheat oven to 350°F. Lightly coat twelve 2½-inch muffin cups with cooking spray. Set aside.

2 In a large bowl stir together flour, granulated sugar, brown sugar, cinnamon, baking powder, salt, and baking soda; set aside.

3 In a medium bowl beat together eggs and milk. Add quinoa, zucchini, applesauce, oil, and vanilla; stir until well mixed. Add quinoa mixture to flour mixture, gently stirring to combine. Spoon batter into prepared muffin cups, filling each about three-fourths full.

4 Bake about 20 minutes or until a toothpick inserted in centers comes out clean. Cool in muffin cups on a wire rack for 5 minutes. Loosen edges; remove cupcakes from muffin cups. Cool on wire rack about 1 hour or until completely cool. Frost with Greek Yogurt Frosting; sprinkle with lemon peel.

GREEK YOGURT FROSTING: In a small bowl whisk together one 6-ounce carton plain fat-free Greek yogurt, 2 tablespoons light agave nectar or 3 tablespoons powdered sugar,* and 1 teaspoon vanilla until combined.

*TEST KITCHEN TIP: We do not recommend using sugar substitutes for this recipe.

**TEST KITCHEN TIP: For 1 cup cooked quinoa, rinse 1/3 cup quinoa. In a small saucepan combine quinoa and 2/3 cup water. Cook according to package directions; cool. Measure out 1 cup. Use any remaining cooked quinoa in salads.

PER SERVING: 167 cal., 6 g total fat (1 g sat. fat), 32 mg chol., 161 mg sodium, 24 g carb. (2 g fiber, 13 g sugars), 5 g pro. Exchanges: 1 starch, 0.5 carb.

Apricot-Vanilla Clafoutis

This pretty dessert is equally good made with fresh peaches or the nectarines shown in the photo. *Pictured on the cover.*

SERVINGS 8 ($^{3}/4$ cup each)
CARB. PER SERVING 18 g or 15 g
PREP 20 minutes
STAND 15 minutes
BAKE 25 minutes
COOL 15 minutes

Nonstick cooking spray

1 vanilla bean, split lengthwise

1 cup evaporated low-fat milk

3 eggs

$^{1}/3$ cup white whole wheat flour or all-purpose flour

$^{1}/4$ cup granulated sugar*

2 tablespoons butter, melted

1 teaspoon vanilla extract

$^{1}/8$ teaspoon salt

12 ounces ripe, yet firm, fresh apricots, sliced

1 teaspoon powdered sugar

1 | Preheat oven to 375°F. Coat the bottom and sides of a 9-inch pie plate with cooking spray; set aside.

2 | With the tip of a sharp knife, scrape seeds from vanilla bean. Place seeds in a small saucepan; add evaporated milk and the vanilla bean pod. Bring to simmering over medium heat; remove from heat. Let stand, uncovered, for 15 minutes. Discard vanilla bean pod.

3 | In a blender or food processor combine eggs, flour, granulated sugar, melted butter, vanilla extract, and salt. Add milk mixture. Cover and blend or process until combined.

4 | Arrange the sliced apricots in the prepared dish. Pour batter over apricots. Bake for 25 to 30 minutes or until puffed and lightly browned. Cool in dish on a wire rack for 15 minutes. Sift the powdered sugar over top. Serve warm.

*SUGAR SUBSTITUTE: Choose Splenda Sugar Blend for Baking. Follow package directions to use product amount equivalent to $^{1}/4$ cup granulated sugar.

PER SERVING: 142 cal., 5 g total fat (2 g sat. fat), 82 mg chol., 124 mg sodium, 18 g carb. (2 g fiber, 14 g sugars), 6 g pro. Exchanges: 0.5 fruit, 0.5 starch, 0.5 medium-fat meat, 1 fat.

PER SERVING WITH SUBSTITUTE: Same as above, except 133 cal., 15 g carb. (10 g sugars).

Salted Caramel Blondies

Crushed potato chips on top give these unconventional brownies a delightful crunch and satisfying bit of salt to go with the sweet.

SERVINGS 28 (1 bar each)
CARB. PER SERVING 22 g
PREP 25 minutes
BAKE 18 minutes

Nonstick cooking spray
1¾ cups packed brown sugar*
⅓ cup butter
¼ cup canola oil
½ cup refrigerated or frozen egg product, thawed
2 teaspoons vanilla
1 cup all-purpose flour
1 cup whole wheat flour
1 teaspoon baking powder
½ teaspoon salt
¼ teaspoon baking soda
½ cup chopped pecans
½ ounce ridged potato chips** (about ¼ cup), coarsely crushed
6 vanilla caramels, unwrapped
1 tablespoon fat-free milk
¼ teaspoon sea salt

PER SERVING: 148 cal., 6 g total fat (2 g sat. fat), 6 mg chol., 115 mg sodium, 22 g carb. (1 g fiber, 15 g sugars), 2 g pro. Exchanges: 0.5 starch, 1 carb., 1 fat.

1 Preheat oven to 350°F. Line a 13×9×2-inch baking pan with foil, extending foil over the edges of the pan; lightly coat foil with cooking spray. In a medium saucepan combine brown sugar, butter, and oil; heat and stir over medium heat until smooth. Remove from heat; cool slightly. Stir in egg and vanilla.

2 In a medium bowl combine the flours, baking powder, the ½ teaspoon salt, and the baking soda. Add the egg mixture to the flour mixture; stir to combine. Stir in pecans. Spread batter evenly in the prepared baking pan. Sprinkle with crushed potato chips.

3 Bake for 18 to 20 minutes or until a toothpick inserted in the center comes out clean. Cool in pan on a wire rack.

4 Meanwhile, in a 1-cup glass measure combine caramels and milk. Microwave on 50 percent power (medium) for 1½ to 2 minutes or until smooth, stirring every 30 seconds. Drizzle mixture over cooled blondies and quickly sprinkle with the sea salt. Using the edges of the foil, lift the uncut blondies out of the pan. Cut into 28 bars.

*TEST KITCHEN TIP: We do not recommend using a sugar substitute for this recipe.

**TEST KITCHEN TIP: Purchase a small snack-size bag of potato chips and measure ¼ cup for this recipe.

Tiramisu Brownie Parfaits

Bring on the yum! The brownie pieces and whipped mixture can be made ahead. Assemble these killer-good parfaits when you're ready.

SERVINGS 6 (1 parfait each)
CARB. PER SERVING 32 g
PREP 20 minutes
BAKE 35 minutes
STAND 10 minutes

Nonstick cooking spray

1 12.35-ounce package sugar-free fudge brownie mix

½ cup unsweetened applesauce

¼ cup refrigerated or frozen egg product, thawed

3 tablespoons canola oil

¼ cup strong brewed coffee

½ of an 8-ounce tub fat-free cream cheese (about ½ cup)

¼ cup fat-free milk

1 1.3-ounce envelope whipped dessert topping mix

½ teaspoon vanilla

1 tablespoon unsweetened cocoa powder

1 tablespoon shaved bittersweet chocolate (optional)

1 Preheat oven to 350°F. Lightly coat an 8×8×2-inch square baking pan with cooking spray. In a medium bowl combine brownie mix, applesauce, egg, and oil, stirring with a wooden spoon until well mixed.

2 Spread batter evenly in the prepared baking pan. Bake about 35 minutes or until a toothpick inserted near the center comes out clean. Cool completely in pan on a wire rack.

3 Cut half of the pan of brownies into 1-inch-square pieces. (Store the remaining half for another use.) Transfer the brownie pieces to a large bowl. Pour the coffee over brownie pieces; toss to coat lightly. Let stand for 10 minutes to allow brownies to soak up the coffee.

4 Meanwhile, in a medium bowl combine cream cheese, milk, dessert topping mix, and vanilla. Beat with an electric mixer on high speed until stiff peaks form (tips stand straight). Cover and chill until ready to assemble parfaits.

5 To serve, layer a few coffee-soaked brownie pieces in the bottom of each of six 4- to 6-ounce glasses. Top each with a spoonful of the whipped topping mixture. Layer with the remaining brownie pieces; top each with another spoonful of the whipped topping. Lightly sift cocoa powder over parfaits. If desired, garnish with shaved chocolate.

PER SERVING: 181 cal., 8 g total fat (2 g sat. fat), 3 mg chol., 240 mg sodium, 32 g carb. (3 g fiber, 5 g sugars), 5 g pro. Exchanges: 2 starch, 1 fat.

5 grams pro.

Strawberry Cheesecake Tartlets

These tartlets are a great make-ahead dessert. You can even freeze them and take out just as many as you want later.

SERVINGS 24 (1 tartlet each)
CARB. PER SERVING 14 g
PREP 25 minutes
BAKE 15 minutes
CHILL 2 hours

1 cup flour

¼ cup granulated sugar*

¼ cup ground toasted almonds

¼ cup butter

1 egg yolk, lightly beaten

2 to 3 tablespoons water

1 4-serving-size package cheesecake-flavor instant pudding and pie filling mix

1 cup evaporated fat-free milk

2 teaspoons vanilla

½ teaspoon almond extract

⅓ cup strawberry spreadable fruit

Sliced strawberries, halved or quartered, and/or toasted sliced almonds

Powdered sugar* (optional)

1 | For tartlet shells, in a medium bowl stir together flour, granulated sugar, and ground almonds. Using a pastry blender, cut in butter until pieces are pea size. In a small bowl combine egg yolk and 2 tablespoons of the water. Gradually stir the yolk mixture into the flour mixture until combined. If necessary, add enough of the remaining 1 tablespoon water, 1 teaspoon at a time, to make a dough that starts to cling together. Gently knead just until smooth; form dough into a ball. If necessary, cover and chill about 1 hour or until dough is easy to handle.

2 | Preheat oven to 350°F. Divide dough into 24 pieces. Shape pieces into balls. Press dough evenly into the bottoms and up the sides of twenty-four 1¾-inch muffin cups. Bake about 15 minutes or until lightly browned. Cool completely in muffin cups on a wire rack. Remove from muffin cups.

3 | For filling, in a medium bowl combine pudding mix, evaporated milk, vanilla, and almond extract. Beat with an electric mixer on medium speed about 2 minutes or until smooth.

4 | Spoon 2 teaspoons of the filling into each tartlet shell. Cover and chill for at least 2 hours or up to 24 hours.

5 | To serve, top each tartlet with about ½ teaspoon of the spreadable fruit and a strawberry slice and/or a few sliced almonds. If desired, dust with powdered sugar.

TO STORE: Layer filled tartlets between sheets of waxed paper in an airtight container; cover. Store in the refrigerator for up to 3 days or freeze for up to 1 month. To serve, thaw tartlets if frozen. Top with spreadable fruit and, if desired, decorate with sliced strawberries and/or toasted sliced almonds.

*TEST KITCHEN TIP: We do not recommend using sugar substitutes for this recipe.

PER SERVING: 86 cal., 3 g total fat (1 g sat. fat), 13 mg chol., 89 mg sodium, 14 g carb. (0 g fiber, 9 g sugars), 2 g pro. Exchanges: 1 starch.

Brown Sugar Peaches

This recipe oozes indulgence. For the most delicious results, we don't recommend using sugar substitutes.

SERVINGS 8 (1 peach half, $^1/_4$ cup frozen yogurt, and 2 teaspoons sauce each)
CARB. PER SERVING 26 g
START TO FINISH 20 minutes

- 4 peaches, halved and pitted
- $^1/_4$ cup packed brown sugar
- $1^1/_2$ teaspoons cornstarch
- 2 tablespoons water
- 3 tablespoons half-and-half
- 1 tablespoon light-color corn syrup
- 1 tablespoon butter
- $^1/_4$ teaspoon vanilla
- 2 cups light vanilla frozen yogurt
- 2 tablespoons coarse raw sugar or packed brown sugar (optional)

PER SERVING: 141 cal., 4 g total fat (2 g sat. fat), 13 mg chol., 61 mg sodium, 26 g carb. (1 g fiber, 14 g sugars), 3 g pro. Exchanges: 1 fruit, 1 carb., 1 fat.

QUICK TIP

If peaches are very large, cut them into quarters before steaming. If desired, slice quarters into slices; fan slices on serving plates before adding frozen yogurt and caramel sauce.

1 Fill a large Dutch oven with water to a depth of 1 inch. Bring water to boiling. Place a steamer basket in the Dutch oven. Place peach halves in the steamer basket. Cover and steam about 5 minutes or until peaches are tender. Remove peaches from steamer basket and place in a large colander to drain.

2 Meanwhile, for caramel sauce, in a small heavy saucepan combine the $^1/_4$ cup brown sugar and the cornstarch. Stir in the water. Stir in half-and-half and corn syrup. Cook and stir until thickened and bubbly (mixture will appear curdled before it thickens). Cook and stir for 2 minutes more. Remove saucepan from heat; stir in butter and vanilla.

3 Serve peaches topped with small scoops of frozen yogurt and drizzled with caramel sauce. If desired, sprinkle with coarse raw sugar.

Lemon Meringue Tarts

The longer these assembled tarts sit, the softer the meringues will become. They'll still taste terrific but will have a softer texture.

SERVINGS 12 (1 tart each)
CARB. PER SERVING 27 g or 16 g
PREP 45 minutes
STAND 30 minutes
BAKE 1 hour 30 minutes
COOL 2 hours
CHILL 1 hour

3 egg whites
¼ teaspoon cream of tartar
¼ teaspoon vanilla
1 cup powdered sugar
3 eggs
¾ cup granulated sugar*
1 tablespoon finely shredded lemon peel
⅓ cup lemon juice
¼ cup butter, cut up
3 ounces reduced-fat cream cheese (Neufchâtel), softened
¾ cup frozen fat-free whipped dessert topping, thawed
1½ cups fresh blackberries

1 Allow egg whites to stand at room temperature for 30 minutes. Line a very large baking sheet with parchment paper or foil. Draw twelve 3- to 3½-inch circles 2 inches apart on the paper or foil; set aside.

2 Preheat oven to 200°F. For meringue, in a medium bowl combine egg whites, cream of tartar, and vanilla. Beat with an electric mixer on medium speed until soft peaks form (tips curl). Add ¾ cup of the powdered sugar, 1 tablespoon at at time, beating on high speed until stiff peaks form (tips stand straight).

3 Spoon or pipe meringue over circles on paper. Bake for 1½ hours. Turn off oven; let meringues dry in oven with door closed for 2 hours. Lift meringues off paper. Transfer to a wire rack.

4 Meanwhile, for lemon curd, in a small saucepan whisk together eggs, the granulated sugar, lemon peel, and lemon juice. Cook and stir over medium heat until mixture comes to a gentle boil. Cook and stir for 2 minutes more. Remove from heat. Add butter pieces, stirring until melted. If desired, press lemon curd through a fine-mesh sieve. Transfer strained mixture to a small bowl. Cover surface with plastic wrap. Chill for at least 1 hour.

5 In a small bowl combine cream cheese, dessert topping, and the remaining ¼ cup powdered sugar; stir until smooth and creamy. Cover and chill until needed.

6 To assemble, place each meringue on a serving plate; spread each with 1 slightly rounded tablespoon of the cream cheese mixture. Add 1 slightly rounded tablespoon of the lemon curd. Top tarts with blackberries. Serve immediately.

*SUGAR SUBSTITUTES: Choose from Splenda Granular, Sweet'N Low bulk or packets, or Truvia Spoonable or packets. Follow package directions to use product amount equivalent to ¾ cup granulated sugar.

PER SERVING: 179 cal., 7 g total fat (4 g sat. fat), 62 mg chol., 92 mg sodium, 27 g carb. (1 g fiber, 24 g sugars), 3 g pro. Exchanges: 2 carb., 1.5 fat.

PER SERVING WITH SUBSTITUTE: Same as above, except 136 cal., 16 g carb. (13 g sugars). Exchanges: 1 carb.

Coconut-Almond Frozen Greek Yogurt with Hot Chocolate Drizzle

Buttermilk helps give this frozen yogurt its wonderful creamy texture. Just enough honey balances the sweet-tart flavors of this dessert.

SERVINGS 11 ($^1/_3$ cup frozen yogurt and 1 tablespoon chocolate topping each)
CARB. PER SERVING 21 g
PREP 15 minutes

- 24 ounces plain fat-free Greek yogurt
- $^1/_2$ cup low-fat buttermilk
- $^1/_3$ cup honey
- $^1/_3$ cup unsweetened shredded coconut, toasted
- $^1/_3$ cup sliced almonds, toasted
- 1 teaspoon coconut extract
- 4 ounces semisweet chocolate, chopped
- 6 tablespoons unsweetened almond milk

Shredded coconut, toasted (optional)

PER SERVING: 153 cal., 6 g total fat (3 g sat. fat), 1 mg chol., 44 mg sodium, 21 g carb. (1 g fiber, 19 g sugars), 7 g pro. Exchanges: 0.5 milk, 1 carb., 1 fat.

1 In a large bowl whisk together yogurt, buttermilk, honey, the $^1/_3$ cup coconut, the almonds, and coconut extract until well mixed.

2 Freeze yogurt mixture in a 1$^1/_2$-quart ice cream freezer according to manufacturer's directions. Transfer yogurt mixture to a freezer container. Cover and freeze for 3 to 4 hours or until firm enough to scoop.

3 Just prior to serving, in a medium saucepan combine chopped chocolate and almond milk. Cook and stir until chocolate is melted and mixture is completely smooth. Drizzle chocolate mixture over scoops of the frozen yogurt.* If desired, garnish with additional toasted coconut.

*TEST KITCHEN TIP: If yogurt is too hard to scoop, microwave on 50 percent power (medium) until soft enough to scoop, checking mixture every 30 seconds to avoid melting.

recipe index

recipe guide

Inside Our Recipes

Precise serving sizes (listed below the recipe title) help you to manage portions.

Ingredients listed as optional are not included in the per-serving nutrition analysis.

When kitchen basics such as ice, salt, black pepper, and nonstick cooking spray are not listed in the ingredients list, they are italicized in the directions.

Ingredients

• Tub-style vegetable oil spread refers to 60% to 70% vegetable oil product.
• Lean ground beef refers to 95% or leaner ground beef.

Nutrition Information

Nutrition facts per serving and food exchanges are noted with each recipe.

Test Kitchen tips and sugar substitutes are listed after the recipe directions.

When ingredient choices appear, we use the first one to calculate the nutrition analysis.

Key to Abbreviations

cal. = calories
sat. fat = saturated fat
chol. = cholesterol
carb. = carbohydrate
pro. = protein

metric information

The charts on this page provide a guide for converting measurements from the U.S. customary system, which is used throughout this book, to the metric system.

Product Differences

Most of the ingredients called for in the recipes in this book are available in most countries. However, some are known by different names. Here are some common American ingredients and their possible counterparts:

* All-purpose flour is enriched, bleached or unbleached white household flour. When self-rising flour is used in place of all-purpose flour in a recipe that calls for leavening, omit the leavening agent (baking soda or baking powder) and salt.
* Baking soda is bicarbonate of soda.
* Cornstarch is cornflour.
* Golden raisins are sultanas.
* Light-color corn syrup is golden syrup.
* Powdered sugar is icing sugar.
* Sugar (white) is granulated, fine granulated, or castor sugar.
* Vanilla or vanilla extract is vanilla essence.

Volume and Weight

The United States traditionally uses cup measures for liquid and solid ingredients. The chart below shows the approximate imperial and metric equivalents. If you are accustomed to weighing solid ingredients, the following approximate equivalents will be helpful.

* 1 cup butter, castor sugar, or rice = 8 ounces = $^{1}/_{2}$ pound = 250 grams
* 1 cup flour = 4 ounces = $^{1}/_{4}$ pound = 125 grams
* 1 cup icing sugar = 5 ounces = 150 grams

Canadian and U.S. volume for a cup measure is 8 fluid ounces (237 ml), but the standard metric equivalent is 250 ml.

1 British imperial cup is 10 fluid ounces.

In Australia, 1 tablespoon equals 20 ml, and there are 4 teaspoons in the Australian tablespoon.

Spoon measures are used for smaller amounts of ingredients. Although the size of the tablespoon varies slightly in different countries, for practical purposes and for recipes in this book, a straight substitution is all that's necessary. Measurements made using cups or spoons always should be level unless stated otherwise.

Common Weight Range Replacements

Imperial / U.S.	Metric
$^{1}/_{2}$ ounce	15 g
1 ounce	25 g or 30 g
4 ounces ($^{1}/_{4}$ pound)	115 g or 125 g
8 ounces ($^{1}/_{2}$ pound)	225 g or 250 g
16 ounces (1 pound)	450 g or 500 g
$1^{1}/_{4}$ pounds	625 g
$1^{1}/_{2}$ pounds	750 g
2 pounds or $2^{1}/_{4}$ pounds	1,000 g or 1 Kg

Oven Temperature Equivalents

Fahrenheit Setting	Celsius Setting*	Gas Setting
300°F	150°C	Gas Mark 2 (very low)
325°F	160°C	Gas Mark 3 (low)
350°F	180°C	Gas Mark 4 (moderate)
375°F	190°C	Gas Mark 5 (moderate)
400°F	200°C	Gas Mark 6 (hot)
425°F	220°C	Gas Mark 7 (hot)
450°F	230°C	Gas Mark 8 (very hot)
475°F	240°C	Gas Mark 9 (very hot)
500°F	260°C	Gas Mark 10 (extremely hot)
Broil	Broil	Grill

Electric and gas ovens may be calibrated using celsius. However, for an electric oven, increase celsius setting 10 to 20 degrees when cooking above 160°C. For convection or forced air ovens (gas or electric), lower the temperature setting 25°F/10°C when cooking at all heat levels.

Baking Pan Sizes

Imperial / U.S.	Metric
9×1$^{1}/_{2}$-inch round cake pan	22- or 23×4-cm (1.5 L)
9×1$^{1}/_{2}$-inch pie plate	22- or 23×4-cm (1 L)
8×8×2-inch square cake pan	20×5-cm (2 L)
9×9×2-inch square cake pan	22- or 23×4.5-cm (2.5 L)
11×7×1$^{1}/_{2}$-inch baking pan	28×17×4-cm (2 L)
2-quart rectangular baking pan	30×19×4.5-cm (3 L)
13×9×2-inch baking pan	34×22×4.5-cm (3.5 L)
15×10×1-inch jelly roll pan	40×25×2-cm
9×5×3-inch loaf pan	23×13×8-cm (2 L)
2-quart casserole	2 L

U.S. / Standard Metric Equivalents

$^{1}/_{8}$ teaspoon = 0.5 ml

$^{1}/_{4}$ teaspoon = 1 ml

$^{1}/_{2}$ teaspoon = 2 ml

1 teaspoon = 5 ml

1 tablespoon = 15 ml

2 tablespoons = 25 ml

$^{1}/_{4}$ cup = 2 fluid ounces = 50 ml

$^{1}/_{3}$ cup = 3 fluid ounces = 75 ml

$^{1}/_{2}$ cup = 4 fluid ounces = 125 ml

$^{2}/_{3}$ cup = 5 fluid ounces = 150 ml

$^{3}/_{4}$ cup = 6 fluid ounces = 175 ml

1 cup = 8 fluid ounces = 250 ml

2 cups = 1 pint = 500 ml

1 quart = 1 litre